# Biblical Strategies to Financial Freedom

# Biblical Strategies to Financial Freedom

## Bringing God's Word to Your Finances

*Dustin B. LaPorte, CFP®*
*and Anissa B. LaPorte, B.S.N., R.N.*

iUniverse, Inc.
New York   Lincoln   Shanghai

Biblical Strategies to Financial Freedom
Bringing God's Word to Your Finances

iUniverse books may be ordered through booksellers or by contacting:

iUniverse
2021 Pine Lake Road, Suite 100
Lincoln, NE 68512
www.iuniverse.com
1-800-Authors (1-800-288-4677)

ISBN-13: 978-0-595-32844-4 (pbk)
ISBN-13: 978-0-595-77644-3 (ebk)
ISBN-10: 0-595-32844-X (pbk)
ISBN-10: 0-595-77644-2 (ebk)

Printed in the United States of America

## We pledge to encourage each other to reach our God-given financial goals.

_____ (signature)

_____ (signature)

_____ (signature)

_____(date)

*"For where two or three come together in my name, there am I with them"* (Matthew 18:20, NIV).

# CONTENTS

# LIFE MISSION

For almost a decade, I have been working to help people implement Biblical financial principles. My wife (Anissa) and I (Dustin) have a life mission to know God and to make Him known by helping and inspiring people to accomplish the dreams God has given them. We are dedicated to learning and sharing financial truths to others.

Together, we started a financial small group ministry at our church and have taught married couples how to implement biblical principles of money management. This book was born out of our experiences teaching the class. Now, our goal is to teach in churches and ministries around the world and help them start financial small groups for God's glory and the edification of His people. If we can be of service to your ministry or organization, we can be reached at…

**Alpha Omega Financial Ministries**
(843) 270-6618

# ACKNOWLEDGMENT

Thank you for purchasing this book. May it be a blessing to you and others you tell about it. The best ideas in the world are worthless if no one knows they exist. Therefore, we are especially thankful for those who are letting people know the power of this book in changing lives for the better.

This book would not be in existence without the encouragement and support from God, family, and friends. We are proud to see it finally completed.

We thank Dan Lempert for placing the teachings into print. Also, we thank our friends for critiquing and editing this book:

Tammie Aycock
Cherryanna Basinger
Kristin Burgess
Michael Kreft
Edie Park
Dr. Rob Pernell
Scott Wells, CFP®
Ellen Wilson
Susan Vaughan
Christa Williams
LaPaula Williams

With their different perspectives, Anissa and I were able to create a book that is easy to read, understand and is life changing.

We would also like to thank Seacoast Church for their prayers and support.

# STRATEGY # 1:

## Know God's Goals for You

# Personal Notes

## Strategy #1: Know God's Goals for You

Team
- Small Group
- Financial Coach and Professional Advisors

Sound Financial Plan
- Goals, Protect, Debt, Accumulate

Financial Checkup

Importance of Money Management

Road Blocks

Goals
- Prayer and Desires
- Time

Ownership
- Master
- Manager
- Faithful Ruler
- Give (Overflowing, Cheerfully, Heavenly Storage, 10% or more, Fool)

Plan

# BUILDING A TEAM

"Two are better than one, because they have a good return for their work: If one falls down, his friend can help him up" (Ecc. 4:9,10, NIV). "Iron sharpeneth iron; so a man sharpeneth the countenance of his friend" (Prov. 27:17, KJV). "Let us not give up meeting together, as some are in the habit of doing, but let us encourage one another" (Hebrews 10:25, NIV). God knows we all need a team to accomplish our goals. That is why we started a financial small group at our church. We call the group *The Courage to Enhance your Marriage and Money.* When we meet, we cover one chapter per meeting by using discussion questions created by the members. Before the meeting, every member is accountable for reading his or her corresponding chapter and completing their assignment:

1st     Do the "The Five Minute Financial Checkup."
2nd    Create a budget.
3rd    Set financial goals.
4th    Complete or review your Will and estate plan.
5th    Be properly insured.
6th    Create a plan to become debt free.
7th    Review your investments.
8th    Review your last year's income tax return.
9th    Create a plan to save for your child's college education.
10th   Create a plan to save for your retirement.
11th   Discover the best investment.

Discussion Questions—While reading a chapter, if a member has a question that he or she wants the group to discuss, then he or she writes the question anonymously on a notecard: "How do you get your spouse to stick to the budget?" "Who would you recommend for...?" "Explain what is a..."

"How can my spouse and I...?" "Give an example how...has made a differ-ence?" At the small group meeting, each member folds and places their note card in a basket. Even if a member does not have a question, he or she still places a blank note card in the basket. To keep it anonymous, mix up the note cards and pass the basket around. Each person draws a note card and reads it for the group to answer. If it is blank then pass to the next person. If a question cannot be answer, then a group member will research it to share at the next meeting. Prayer Requests—At the end of the meeting, each member writes on a new notecard his or her name and prayer request. The men will place their prayers on one side of a table and women on the other side. One-by-one the men will draw from the male side and the women from the female side. Whoever's name you receive, you commit to pray for that person until the next meeting.

We all need at least one person that is there to give us encouragement, accountability, wisdom, and focus to accomplish our God given goals. That person could be a financial professional or it could be a close friend. We like to call that person a
Financial Coach.

My Financial Coach is _____.

# FINANCIAL CHECKUP

This book is based on the financial planning model which starts with the plan. Each strategy builds upon the other. The first strategy is to ask yourself...

What is God's will and plan for you? God has a plan for each of us. God told Jeremiah, "'I know the plans I have for you', declares the LORD, 'plans to prosper you and not to harm you, plans to give you hope and a future. Then you will call upon me and come and pray to me, and I will listen to you. You will seek me and find me when you seek me with all your heart'" (Jer. 29:11-13, NIV). The next strategy is to protect your assets and income. The third strategy is to eliminate all your high interest rate debt. This type of debt can greatly hinder you from fulfilling the dreams God gives you. The final strategy is to save for your long-term goals.

The Bible teaches to "be sure you know the condition of your flocks, give careful attention to your herds; for riches do not endure forever" (Prov. 27:23-24, NIV). What is the condition of your flock? Taking the *FIVE MINUTE FINANCIAL CHECKUP* will help you do a reality check. Notice on the left side is a box. I call it the "To Do" box. If it is something you need to do then mark it and turn to the chapter that corresponds with the question. Once you have completed the "checkup", I encourage you to share it with someone who will hold you accountable to accomplish the "To Do" list. For those who are married, I want to emphasize the importance of sharing the "Checkup" together. By having a common vision and direction for your family's finances, you and your spouse can make better financial decisions. Another great resource is the *General Recommendation CheckList*, found in the back of this book.

# FIVE MINUTE FINANCIAL CHECKUP

## STRATEGY #1:
## Know God's Goals for You

☐ I have a written plan for achieving my financial goals (retirement, college fund, eliminating debt, etc.).
☐ Yes      ☐ No

## STRATEGY #2:
## Protect Assets and Income

☐ I have a written Savings & Spending Plan.
☐ Yes      ☐ No

☐ I have the equivalent of 4 to 8 months of living expenses in my bank savings account or money market and/or a line of credit for major emergencies.
☐ Yes      ☐ No

☐ I have a current valid estate plan (Will, trust(s), power of attorney, Living Will, etc.) designed to effectively transfer wealth, minimize cost, and reduce hassle.
☐ Yes      ☐ No

☐ I have updated the beneficiaries on all my accounts (life insurance, IRAs, 401k, joint accounts with rights of survivorship, etc.).
☐ Yes      ☐ No

☐ When I die, my executor can easily find and obtain the necessary documents.
☐ Yes      ☐ No

☐ I have enough life insurance and investments that upon my death, the proceeds will pay off all debt and provide for those who are dependent on my income (college fund, income, day care, etc.).
☐ Yes ☐ No

☐ Due to my investments and insurance, I can still financially survive and reach my financial goals even if I

| | |
|---|---|
| ☐ became disabled | ☐ Yes ☐ No |
| ☐ needed long-term care for life | ☐ Yes ☐ No |
| ☐ received a large medical bill | ☐ Yes ☐ No |
| ☐ lost a lawsuit against me | ☐ Yes ☐ No |
| ☐ had valuable property lost, destroyed or stolen | ☐ Yes ☐ No |

## STRATEGY #3:
## Eliminate High Interest Rate Debt

☐ Every month I pay off my credit cards before I receive a finance charge.
☐ Yes ☐ No

☐ I have a written plan for becoming debt free.
☐ Yes ☐ No

# STRATEGY #4:
## Accumulate for Goals

☐ I have matched my goals with my investments and risk tolerance.
☐ Yes      ☐ No

☐ Most of my investments are insured or diversified through a variety of assets, managers, and styles.
☐ Yes      ☐ No

☐ I have a good understanding of how to determine my federal income taxes.
☐ Yes      ☐ No

☐ I use tax-advantaged ways to save for college (ROTH IRA, UGMA, Coverdell Education Savings Account, etc.).
☐ Yes      ☐ No

☐ I contribute the maximum my company's retirement plan matches.
☐ Yes      ☐ No

☐ I use tax-advantaged accounts to save for retirement (ROTH, Traditional IRA, Annuity, Cash Value Life Insurance, 401k, SEP, SIMPLE IRA, etc.).
☐ Yes      ☐ No

☐ I am daily investing in the things that matter the most in life.
☐ Yes      ☐ No

# FINANCIAL GOALS

"Commit to the LORD whatever you do, and your plans will succeed.
The LORD works out everything for his
own ends…"
(Proverbs 16:3-4, NIV).

Why Do You Think the Bible Says more about managing money than it does about heaven and hell combined?

Can it be…your spending habits reveal what matters the most to you: "For where your treasure is, there your heart will be also" (Mat. 6:21, KJV)?

Can it be…better financial management leads to financial freedom and the ability to contribute to the things that matter the most to you: God, family, friends, etc.?

Can it be…God is concerned about your family life because financial mismanagement and the lack of communication are leading destroyers of most marriages?

Why is proper money management important to you?

Whatever the reason, if it is important to God, then it should be important to you!

# Road Blocks

Before we begin this journey together, let's look at the financial mistakes others have made and learn from them.

**Procrastination/Laziness:** "Lazy hands make a man poor, but diligent hands bring wealth. He who gathers crops in summer is a wise son, but he who sleeps during harvest is a disgraceful son" (Proverbs 10:4-5, NIV). "Therefore to him that knoweth to do good, and doeth [it] not, to him it is sin" (James 4:17, KJV).

**Failure to Pray and Plan:** "Whatsoever we ask, we receive of {God}, because we keep his commandments, and do those things that are pleasing in his sight" (1 John 3:22, KJV). "Unless the LORD builds the house, its builders labor in vain...In vain you rise early and stay up late, toiling for food to eat—for while they sleep he provides for those he loves" (Psalms 127:1-2, NIV). Where God guides, He provides. It does not mean it is going to be easy, but it will be faith building. Look at the plans God gave Noah, Moses, Jesus, Abraham, and King David. They knew what God had called them to do. The plan was never easy to accomplish. Many times it was impossible to accomplish. Through God's power and strength, the plan was established and fulfilled. Lack of Commitment: We must do more than just talk: "In all labor there is profit: but the talk of the lips {leads} only to {poverty}" (Proverbs 14:23, KJV). "Commit to the Lord whatever you do, and your plans will succeed" (Proverbs 16:3, NIV).

**Lack of Knowledge:** "My people are destroyed from lack of knowledge" (Hosea 4:6, KJV). "Without counsel, purposes {plans} are disappointed: but in the multitude of counselors they are established {real, accomplished, completed, and fulfilled}" (Proverbs 15:22, KJV). Pride keeps us from seeking professional help. The fact is we need each other.

# Time Is Money

Most people don't plan to fail. They simply fail to plan. When planning, it is important to know where you want to go before you try to get there. That is why it is so crucial that you spend time with God.

"Delight thyself also in the LORD; and he shall give thee the desires of thine heart. Commit thy way unto the LORD; trust also in him; and he shall bring [it] to pass. Rest in the LORD, and wait patiently for..." (Psalms 37:4,5,7, KJV).

Delight yourself in the LORD, worship, pray, enjoy His love, and His desires will become your desires. Through fellowship with God, He plants inside you the dreams and goals He desires and wills you to accomplish. Plus, He empowers you to accomplish them. It is not easy. Look at the lives of every famous person of faith in the Bible (Abraham, Noah, Moses, Joseph, Joshua, King David, Daniel, Paul, Peter, John, John the Baptist). Many of the things God called them to do were extremely difficult or impossible to accomplish without God's intervention.

"Being confident of this very thing, that he which hath begun a good work in you will perform [it] until the day of Jesus Christ" (Philippians 1:6, KJV).

Failure to spend time with God, distorts your desires and prayers. "You want something but don't get it. You kill and covet, but you cannot have what you want. You quarrel and fight. You do not have, because you do not ask God. When you ask, you do not receive, because you ask with wrong motives, that you may spend what you get on your pleasures" (James 4:2-3, NIV).

Discover God's will and align your life with it. Pray and seek counsel. If time is money, then make sure you are using your time wisely. Write down your personal and financial goals. Then look at your daily activities and remove those activities that are not aligned with your obligations and goals. There are a lot of good things you can do, but the question you need to ask yourself is, "Is this what God wants me to be doing at this time?"

*The problem with lacking a clear direction is that it is easy to lose valuable time doing unproductive activities.*

# Know the Master of Money

If you want to know how to master money, develop a relationship with the Master of money, the Master of everything.

"Everything under heaven belongs to [God]" (Job 41:11, NIV).

"Both riches and honour [come from God], and thou reignest over all; and in thine hand [is] power and might; and in thine hand [it is] to make great, and to give strength unto all." (1 Chr. 29:12-13, KJV).

"Now to him who is able to do immeasurably more than all we ask or imagine, according to his power that is at work within us…" (Eph. 3:20, NIV).

God is the creator and owner of everything, and we are just managers of His resources. He is our provider.

Some people mistakenly think that financial management is only for the rich. If that is true, then why does God teach since "thou hast been faithful over a few things, I will make thee ruler over many things…" (Mat. 25:22, KJV)? If God cannot trust you with the little He has given you, why should He ever give you more?

For example, sometimes when people are given a low interest, low monthly payment loan to consolidate all their debts, they soon obtain another credit card and start their destructive spending patterns all over again. You must treat the problem, not just the symptom, or the destructive spending habits will continue and no amount of money will ever be enough. Until God can trust you with the little He has given you, do not expect a lot.

Some who are wealthy believe they do not need to be prudent in financial management. In fact, the more you have, the more God expects of you.

"For unto whomsoever much is given, of him shall be much required" (Luke 12:24, KJV).

By having a relationship with God you learn to manage money in ways that are more beneficial than you can imagine. The benefits go beyond the now and into eternity.

# Honor God

**The most important step in money management is to know and honor the one who provides all our wealth:**
"Both riches and honor come from God" (1Chr. 29:12, NIV).

"Honor the LORD with your wealth…then your barns will be filled to overflowing, and your vats will brim over with new wine" (Prov. 3:9-10, NIV)

"'Bring ye all the tithes {literally means 10%} into the storehouse…prove me now herewith,' saith the LORD of hosts, 'if I will not open you the windows of heaven, and pour you out a blessing, that [there shall] not [be room] enough [to receive it].'" (Mal. 3:10, KJV)

"Give, and it shall be given unto you; good measure, pressed down, and shaken together, and running over…For with the same measure that [you use] it shall be measured to you again" (Luke 6:38, KJV)

"So let each one give as he purposes in his heart, not grudgingly or of necessity; for God loves a cheerful giver…" (2 Cor. 9:7, NIV)

"He who sows sparingly will also reap sparingly, and he who sows bountifully will also reap bountifully." (2 Cor. 9:6, NIV).

**Invest your time, talents, and wealth into helping others:**
"…store up for yourselves treasures in heaven where moth and rust do not destroy, and where thieves do not break in and steal. For where your treasure is, there your heart will be also'" (Mat. 6:19-21, NIV).

"Wealth is worthless in the day of wrath…One man gives freely, yet gains even more; another withholds unduly, but comes to poverty….whoever trusts in riches will fall" (Prov. 11:4,24,25,28, KJV).

**God is more concerned about the condition of your heart than the dollar amount you give:**

"Jesus saw the rich putting their gifts into the temple treasury. He also saw a poor widow put in two very small copper coins. 'I tell you the truth', he said, 'this poor widow has put in more than all the others. All these people gave their gifts out of their wealth; but she out of her poverty put in all she had to live on.'" (Luke 21:1-4, NIV).

She gave more than 10%. She gave it all. Would you?

**Be rich toward God:**

"'This is what I'll do…I will store all my grain and my goods.' And I'll say to myself, 'you have plenty of good things laid up for many years. Take life easy; eat, drink and be merry.' But God said to him, 'you fool! This very night your life will be demanded from you. Then who will get what you have prepared for yourself?' This is how it will be with anyone who stores up things for himself but is <u>not rich toward God</u>."(Luke 12:18-21, NIV).

There is nothing wrong with saving and living off your investments as long as you are rich towards God. Supporting your church ministry is a top priority. What you do not have in money to give, you should be making up the difference as a part-time job helping your church do maintenance, yard work, building, ushering, teaching, working in the nursery, or whatever they need.

# Making the Plan

Once you have your goals listed, I would encourage you to find out what you need to do in order to reach your financial goals. Find someone to be your financial coach to keep you accountable in successfully reaching your goals. A Financial Coach can be a close friend or a financial professional. If you are reluctant to reveal your finances or financial troubles with a friend then hire a CERTIFIED FINANCIAL PLANNER™ professional to work with you.

Besides confidentiality, a CERTIFIED FINANCIAL PLANNER™ professional can make the planning process easier for you by using his/her extensive experience and knowledge to lessen your chances of making costly mistakes. Besides having a financial coach, you need a financial calculator to help you make your plans. The internet has a wide variety of free web-based financial calculators to help you calculate how much life insurance you will need, how much money you will need to save monthly for goals, etc.

What are the goals and dreams God has put into your heart?

☐   **Having children**
☐   **Savings for your retirement**
☐   **Giving more to Missions**
☐   **Becoming debt free**
☐   **Savings for your children's college fund**
☐   _____
☐   _____
☐   _____

# Web-based Financial Calculators*

Here are samples of financial resources at the Kiplinger's web site www.kiplinger.com/tools:

## TAXES:
Tax outlook calculator
How much will a new mortgage reduce my taxes?
How much will a home-equity loan reduce my taxes?

## MORTGAGES:
How much will my home payments be?
How much will adjustable rate payments be?
Which is better: fixed or adjustable?
Should I pay points to lower the rate?
Which is better: 15 or 30-year mortgage?
Am I better off refinancing?
How much can you spend for housing?
What will my refinancing costs be?
How advantageous are extra payments?
What will my tax savings be?

## CHILDREN:
How much will it cost to raise a child?
100 best values in public colleges.
Top 100 values in private colleges.

## INVESTING:
How will taxes and inflation affect my savings?
What is my return if I sell now?
Which is better: Regular IRA or Roth IRA?

Here are some of the financial calculators at the CNN Money's website (cgi.money.cnn.com/tools/):

DEBT:
Debt Reduction Planner.
Ideal Budget.

COLLEGE:
College savings planner.
College cost finder.

YOUR HOME:
What will your payments be?
Are two homes better than one?
Cost of Living.
Shop for mortgage.

INVESTING:
How fast will your savings grow?
Retirement Planner.
How much will you need for retirement?
Millionaire calculator.
Rate of return calculator.

*\*If legal, financial, tax or other professional advice is required, those services should be provided by an accredited and licensed advisor who can advise you on your specific needs. The advice and views expressed from these websites may be different from the views and advice Anissa and Dustin LaPorte would provide. Anissa and Dustin LaPorte cannot guarantee the accuracy of the websites, nor can Anissa and Dustin LaPorte guarantee these websites still offer their services.*

# STRATEGY # 2:
## Protect Assets and Income

# PERSONAL NOTES

## Strategy #2: Protect Assets and Income

Budget
- Spending Plan
- Priorities
- Weekly 4.5

Emergency Fund
- 4 to 8 Months
- $100,000
- Line of Credit

Estate Plan
- 9 Months
- Expenses/Resources
- Asset Transfer
- Guardian/Control
- Will
- Probate

Disabled
- Power of Attorney/Living Will
- Burial

Estate Transfer
- Beneficiaries
- Retirement Accounts, Joint Accounts, Life Insurance, etc.
  - Supersede Will and avoid probate
- Joint Accounts
  - Problem with rights of survivorship
- Estate Taxes
- Trust
- Family Business

Insurance
- Appropriate Insurance Coverage
- Worksheet

# BUDGET AND EMERGENCY PLAN

"Be sure you know the condition of your flocks, give careful attention to
your herds; for riches do not endure forever"
(Proverbs 27: 23-24, NIV).

Condition of Your Flock "Be sure to know the condition of your flocks,
give careful attention to your herds because riches do not endure forever"
(Prov. 27:23-24, NIV). This proverb was written by King Solomon, one of
the wisest and wealthiest individuals during his lifetime. You probably do
not own a herd, but you do have financial resources. One of the best ways
to know the condition of your finances is to follow a spending plan
(budget).

A spending plan gives you the freedom to know how much money you can
spend without sacrificing your future. Throughout the centuries, people
have successfully budgeted by following this simple strategy:

• Set aside money each pay period for obligations and goals.

• With the left over income, pay yourself a weekly cash allowance to spend
freely.

• If you do not have enough money to purchase an item, then wait until
you do.

It is a simple and powerful strategy to achieve your financial goals. Even
the Apostle Paul, over a thousand years ago, knew that people needed a
savings and spending plan to help them prepare for the future. "On the
first day of every week, each one of you should set aside a sum of money in

keeping with his income, saving it up, so that when I come no collections will have to be made" (1 Cor. 16:2, NIV). Sound familiar?

What is your spending plan?

Spend first and hope for the rest?

Or is it, save first for your priorities and obligations (tithing, saving, investing, bills, taxes, etc.), then spend what is left?

How you spend your money is a testimony of what matters the most to you. If someone examined your checkbook and credit card statements what would they learn about you? By following a spending plan, you can direct your financial resources to the things that matter most and help prevent you from overspending.

Remember that…

"Godliness with contentment is great gain" (1 Tim. 6:6, NIV); and

"The fruit of the Spirit is…
                            patience…
                                   and self control" (Gal. 5:22-23, NIV).

# Budget for the Future

If you need assistance in creating a spending plan, you can use the budget worksheet or go to this website:

www.kiplinger.com/tools/budget.html

Before you begin your budget, look at your past banking statements, credit card bills, and cash receipts to determine your spending habits and estimate your expenditures. This helps remind you of the bills that may come once a year like property taxes, licenses, and homeowner's dues. These are the bills that like to sneak up on you if you forget about them.

Converting expenditures into monthly amounts makes it easier to manage. Annual, semiannual, and quarterly expenses can be converted to monthly expenses by taking the dollar amount needed to pay the bill and dividing it by the months until the bill is due.

Converting weekly expenditures into monthly amounts requires some adjustment. Many believe there are roughly four weeks in a month. Thus, they take weekly expenses and multiply them by four to estimate their monthly expenditures. The problem is 4 weeks times 12 (twelve meaning 12 months) equals 48 weeks. However, there are 52 weeks in a year, not 48 weeks. To play it safe, for weekly expenses multiply it by 4.5 to estimate the monthly expenditures. It is better to over budget than under budget.

# Monthly $pending Plan Worksheet

We encourage you to fill out this *Monthly Spending Plan* worksheet. Convert all income and expenses to monthly averages. Take your *Monthly Gross Income* and subtract it from all other monthly expenses. Your *Monthly Gross Income* needs to be greater than your *Monthly Expenses*. If not then you need to look for ways to lower your expenses or increase your income.

**TOTAL MONTHLY GROSS INCOME**                    $ _____

Salary & Earned Income                    $ _____
Child Support & Alimony                    $ _____
Pension & Social Security                    $ _____
Rental Income                    $ _____
Other_____                    $ _____
Other_____                    $ _____

**TOTAL LIABILITIES**                    $ _____

Mortgage Payment or Rent                    $ _____
Vacation Home Mortgage                    $ _____
Vacation Home taxes                    $ _____
Automobile Loan(s)                    $ _____
Personal Loans/Charge Accts                    $ _____
Child Support & Alimony                    $ _____
Other_____                    $ _____
Other_____                    $ _____

## TOTAL TAXES $ _____

Federal Income Taxes         $ _____
State & Intangible Taxes       $ _____
You (FICA & Medicare)        $ _____
Spouse (FICA & Medicare)     $ _____
Residential Taxes             $ _____
Property Taxes               $ _____
Other_____     $ _____
Other_____     $ _____

## TOTAL INSURANCE COST $ _____

Life Insurance               $ _____
Health Insurance            $ _____
Disability Income Ins.        $ _____
Auto Insurance              $ _____
Home Owners Insurance     $ _____
Other_____     $ _____
Other_____     $ _____
Other_____     $ _____
Other_____     $ _____
Other_____     $ _____
Other_____     $ _____

## TOTAL TRANSPORTATION COST $ _____

Gas and Oil                 $ _____
Maintenance and Repair      $ _____
License, Registration         $ _____
Public Transportation        $ _____
Other_____     $ _____
Other_____     $ _____

## TOTAL MONTHLY SAVINGS $ _____

Emergency Funds $ _____
Savings Account $ _____
Retirement Funds $ _____
College Funds $ _____
Vacation Fund $ _____
Other_____ $ _____
Other_____ $ _____
Other_____ $ _____
Other_____ $ _____
Other_____ $ _____
Other_____ $ _____

## TOTAL CHARITY CONTRIBUTIONS $ _____

Tithes & Offerings $ _____
Charitable $ _____
Other_____ $ _____
Other_____ $ _____

## TOTAL HOUSEHOLD EXPENSES $ _____

Food $ _____
Clothing $ _____
Doctor & Dentist $ _____
Prescription Drugs $ _____
Professional Fees $ _____
Education Expenses $ _____
Day Care $ _____
Personal Care $ _____
Electricity, Gas, Fuel $ _____
Telephone $ _____
Water & Water Conditioners $ _____

Garbage and Pest Control $ _____
Home Maintenance/Repair $ _____
Security Systems $ _____
Home Furnishings $ _____
Entertainment & Hobbies $ _____
Veterinarian & Pet Care $ _____
Books, Magazines, & Paper $ _____
Club Dues $ _____
Vacation and Travel $ _____
Children's Allowances $ _____
Gifts $ _____
Other_____ $ _____
Other_____ $ _____

**TOTAL MONTHLY GROSS INCOME**    $ _____

**TOTAL MONTHLY EXPENSES**    $ _____

Your *Monthly Gross Income* needs to be greater than your *Monthly Expenses*. If not then you need to look for ways to lower your expenses or increase your income.

# Emergency Fund/Line of Credit

"Give portions to seven, yes to eight, for you do not know what disaster may come upon the land" (Ecc. 11:2, NIV).

You need an emergency fund because you never know when a financial disaster will come your way. Usually you need the equivalent of 4 to 8 months of living expenses in an insured FDIC bank savings or money market account. These types of accounts will not make you rich; they pay a very low interest rate. You may be asking yourself, "If they pay such a low interest, then why should I invest my money in them?" The problem is most high return investments fluctuate in value and are not insured. Regardless of market conditions, a FDIC insured bank savings account or bank money market account is insured up to $100,000 per person per banking institution with few exceptions. It is money you can count on to be there when you need it the most.

Do you have an emergency fund in place?

"A prudent man sees danger and takes refuge, but the simple keep going and suffer for it. Humility and the fear of the LORD bring wealth and honor and life" (Prov. 22:3-4).

Having money in the bank is great for emergencies, but what if you do not have enough money in the bank for emergencies? If you lose your job, how are you going to pay your bills? You can draw unemployment, but will that be enough? You can use your savings and investments. You can sell assets like your house, car, furniture, etc. You could reduce your living expenses. You can ask your church, friends, and family to help. As an effort to survive, you can borrow.

However, who will lend you money when you have no income? This is why it is important to establish a line of credit before you ever need it.

Think of a line of credit as an insurance policy instead of a tool to buy things. It is primarily for survival (EMERGENCIES) and not for luxury...

For instance, if you are in danger of losing your house, you can use your line of credit to pay the mortgage until you sell your house. You could use any of the profits you make from selling your house to pay off the line of credit. There are all types of lines of credit. The type I received from my bank came with a checkbook. At my bank there is no cost to have it, as long as I do not use it. It is like having insurance that is free unless you use it. What a great safety net for emergencies!

What is your safety net?

# ESTATE PLAN

"A good man leaves an inheritance for his children's children" (Proverbs 13:22, NIV).

Through proper estate planning, you can protect your family's estate from unnecessary taxes, fees, and hassles. Estate tax is the tax that your estate pays when you die. With few exceptions, at death, the estate has only 9 months to pay in cash any estate tax that is due. Also, there are burial, executor, probate, attorney expenses, and other costs. Easily, probate expenses can range from 4% to 7% of an estate's total value plus another 1.5 to 2% in court costs (American Estate Planning Attorney Directory, 2003). How will the estate pay these expenses, especially if there is not enough cash in the estate? The family home, investments, and precious heirlooms may have to be sold. Additionally, due to time constraints and market conditions, these assets may have to be liquidated below their market value. Without a valid Will, the state intestacy laws decide who receives your personal assets and who will take care of your minor children.

Dustin and Anissa LaPorte are not tax advisors. To understand your personal tax situation completely, always consult your tax advisor. The information provided in this book is based on January 2004 tax laws. Tax laws are subject to change.

# Why estate planning?

- To reduce your heirs' estate taxes and other associated taxes and fees.
- To plan for the cash and life insurance needs to settle the estate.
- To provide proper and efficient transfer of assets to your heirs.
- To have resources or insurance set aside to provide for those who are still dependent upon your income.
- To direct who will take care of your children, parents, pets, etc.
- To specify who will be the executor of the estate.
- To use certain trusts to maintain control over the assets and protect your family.
- To use a valid Will to allow your will to be done on earth while you're in heaven.

What legacy and wealth will you leave behind to those you love? Will they remember you as a prudent and wise person? Do you desire that most of your wealth go to those you love and to the charities you support—or to taxes? Without planning, the IRS may be the main beneficiary of your estate.

Why do you need a Will?

If you are unable to mentally or physically transact business, who will have the legal authority to act in your behalf (write checks, make withdrawals, sell your assets and investments, etc.)? If you are terminally ill or injured, do you want life support machines to keep you alive, and for how long? What should be done with your body after you die? A competent attorney can create legal documents to address these concerns and more.

You may want to write down your assets, stating the estimated value of each asset, and who you would like to inherit it. This helps with estate valuation. Also, it can assist in making insurance claims.

Probate is when the court system validates and makes public the Will of the deceased. Assets inside a trust avoid the probate process and do not become public knowledge. This is a private way of transferring assets.

It is surprising that 58% of all Americans do not have a written Will (Wall Street Journal, 2004). There is no excuse why people cannot have a Will. Especially when companies like Pre-Paid Legal Services®, Inc. offer their members access to lawyers to do their Will at no additional charge; a Will that meets most Americans' needs with free yearly reviews and updates for members. Also, they offer Wills for other covered family members; however, they may incur a small fee. To find out more about the plan that is offered in your state visit their website (www.prepaidlegal.com).

For more information on estate planning refer to:

www.estateplanninglink.com

www.laweasy.com

or/and your estate tax attorney.

> "A valid Will allows your will to be done
> on earth while you're in heaven."

# Estate Transfer

The named beneficiaries on your life insurance policies, IRAs, joint accounts with rights of survivorship, retirement accounts, supersede a Will and avoid probate. As a result, there is a danger for those who do not keep their beneficiary information current. What if it is written in your Will that all your assets should transfer to your spouse, but your parents are still the beneficiaries of your life insurance and retirement accounts? When you die, the life insurance and IRA's proceeds will transfer to your parents even though your Will says differently.

Example of a problem with joint accounts with rights of survivorship: You have three children, two sons and one daughter, and want your assets to be divided equally upon your death. Your daughter lives near you, and your sons live in other states. In case you became incapacitated, you want your daughter to have access to your money to act in your behalf. So you convert all your accounts to be jointly owned with your daughter with rights of survivorship. When you die, these assets avoid probate, automatically transfer, and belong entirely to your daughter, and will not be divided equally among your children. Your daughter may try to correct the problem by gifting the joint assets. However, in doing so, she may incur a gift tax.

There are potential tax benefits in naming a beneficiary on certain types of retirement accounts such as an annuity or IRA. The beneficiary may be able to stretch the payment of the proceeds over his or her life expectancy, thus deferring part of the taxes due and allowing maximum tax deferred growth.

Make sure your Will and other important documents can easily be found and obtained. Your heirs need to know about your life insurance and financial assets. If no one knows you have insurance coverage, who is going to tell the life insurance carrier that you died? What if the insurance carrier cancels the policy since they were no longer receiving payments?

Many people store their Will and other important documents in a safety deposit box at their bank. Their Will usually indicates who will be their personal representative of their estate. The problem is, in most states, as soon as you die, your own personal safety deposit box is sealed and can only be opened by the personal representative of your estate. If your Will is locked in the safety deposit box, then how can it be opened? Only by a court order! Needless to say, this can cause a major problem and delay in settling your estate.

# You're Richer than You Think

You may believe that you do not have a large enough estate to be concerned about estate taxes. You might be surprised! Your estate includes your assets such as your business, annuities, investments, artwork, and real estate. It also includes the life insurance death benefit proceeds.

The government does allow you to subtract from your estate your debts, charitable gifts, tax credits, other deductions, and the assets that all transferred to your spouse. The remainder of the estate is subject to estate taxation.

> + Assets (real estate, investments, art work, jewelry, etc.)
> + Life Insurance Proceeds
>
> - Debts
> - Assets Given to Charity
> - Assets Given to Your Spouse
> - Attorney and Court Fees
> - Burial Expense
> - Other Deductions
>
> = Taxable Estate

Not everyone will have to pay estate taxes because the government provides a tax credit. As of the year 2004, most taxable estates less than $1.5 million will not have to pay estate taxes because of the Unified Estate Tax Credit.

The estate tax rules require diligent monitoring because they frequently change. If you find yourself subject to an estate tax situation, I encourage you to hire an estate tax lawyer to create and monitor your own estate plan.

For a current tax chart visit:
www.statefarm.com/insuranc/life/taxgone.htm

For an estimated estate tax calculation visit:
www.statefarm.com/jscript/estate.htm

To help calculate your estate taxes you can visit:
www.turbotax.com/planning/calculators.html

# 2004 Unified Estate & Gift Tax Schedule

Once you determine the amount that is subject to estate taxes then look at the current Unified Estate and Gift Tax Schedule to determine the tax owed. The estate tax and gift tax schedules are the same.

If your taxable estate is $1,500,000 in the year 2004, then your estate tax due is $555,800. Most people are eligible for an estate tax credit of $555,800. Even though you may owe $555,800 in estate taxes to the federal government, the estate tax bill is zero due to the estate tax credit. In 2004, the tax credit is up to $555,800 which is the equivalent to an estate of $1,500,000. Currently, the applicable credit amount is scheduled to gradually increase over time.

As a side note, for gift tax purposes in years 2004 and 2005 the Unified Credit is $345,800, the applicable exclusion amount is $1,000,000. For estate tax purposes in years 2004 and 2005 the Unified Credit is $555,800 and the applicable exclusion amount is $1,500,000. With time, the amount that can pass to an heir's estate tax-free will change; thus, so should your plans.

**Unified Estate Tax Credit**
**Equivalent Schedule** (as of year 2004)

| Year | Equivalent Estate |
| --- | --- |
| 2002–2003 | $1,000,000 |
| 2004–2005 | $1,500,000 |
| 2006–2008 | $2,000,000 |
| 2009 | $3,500,000 |
| 2010 | N/A |
| 2011 | $1,000,000 |

# How to Determine Estate Taxes

In 2004, what would be the estate tax on a single person who died with a $3,000,000 taxable estate? **STEP 1:** Take $3,000,000 and subtract $2,000,000, which equals $1,000,000 (the amount above the $2,000,000). **STEP 2:** Multiply $1,000,000 by the 48% estate tax, which equals $480,000. **STEP 3:** Now add the $780,800 for a grand total of $1,260,000 due on a $3,000,000 estate. **STEP 4:** Then subtract the $555,800 tax credit. $1,260,000 minus $555,800 tax credit equals the required estate tax due of $704,200.

| Taxable estate | | Tax before credit | | |
|---|---|---|---|---|
| | But not | | | On excess |
| Over | more than | Pay | Plus % | more than |
| $0 | $10,000 | $0 | 18% | $0 |
| $10,000 | $20,000 | $1,800 | 20% | $10,000 |
| $20,000 | $40,000 | $3,800 | 22% | $20,000 |
| $40,000 | $60,000 | $8,200 | 24% | $40,000 |
| $60,000 | $80,000 | $13,000 | 26% | $60,000 |
| $80,000 | $100,000 | $18,200 | 28% | $80,000 |
| $100,000 | $150,000 | $23,800 | 30% | $100,000 |
| $150,000 | $250,000 | $38,800 | 32% | $150,000 |
| $250,000 | $500,000 | $70,800 | 34% | $250,000 |
| $500,000 | $750,000 | $155,800 | 37% | $500,000 |
| $750,000 | $1,000,000 | $248,300 | 39% | $750,000 |
| $1,000,000 | $1,250,000 | $345,800 | 41% | $1,000,000 |
| $1,250,000 | $1,500,000 | $448,300 | 43% | $1,250,000 |
| $1,500,000 | $2,000,000 | $555,800 | 45% | $1,500,000 |
| $2,000,000 | and above | $780,800 | 48% | $2,000,000 |

# Give it Away

There are ways to reduce or eliminate estate taxes. One way to avoid estate taxes is to give your estate to a charity. If you try to give away your estate to family and friends while you are alive, the gifts may be subject to gift taxes. As of the year 2004, a person can give up to $11,000 per calendar year per person without incurring a gift tax. If you distribute your estate while you are alive, you may miss out on an important tax break: a step-up in cost basis. Your cost basis is what you paid for the asset. It is used to determine how much you need to pay in capital gains. For example, you bought an investment for $10,000 and gave it to your daughter who eventually sold it for $100,000. Since the cost basis was $10,000 and she sold it for $100,000, the profit would be $90,000 which would be subject to the capital gains tax. If she had inherited the investment at $100,000, for tax purposes the original price paid for the investment (cost basis $10,000) is reset to the inherit value of the investment ($100,000). If she sold it for $100,000, there would be no capital gain because her new cost basis is $100,000. That is what we mean by step-up in cost basis. However, the cost basis could step-down if inherited at a price below its original purchase price. It is important to note that in 2010, the government is planning to eliminate the estate tax, and lower the gift tax rate. They plan to limit the amount you can "step-up".

In 2010, the surviving spouse will be able to receive up to a $4,300,000 increase in cost basis on the deceased spouse's assets transferred to the surviving spouse. The deceased assets transferred to a non-spouse will receive up to a $1,300,000 increase in cost basis. After 2010, it is unsure if this will become a permanent tax law or if it will be eliminated and return to pre-2010 estate tax laws. It is important to note that not all investments get a step-up or step-down in cost basis. Please check with your tax advisor for your situation.

When transferring assets to your grandchildren, be careful of the generation-skipping transfer tax (GSTT). A skip person is anyone more than one generation removed from the donor or deceased. The GSTT is not imposed if you do not have a generation to skip. For example, your grand-children could inherit your estate if your children are deceased. The GSTT is equal to the highest current unified federal estate and gift tax rate (48% in 2004). Every person is permitted to skip a generation and distribute up to $1.5 million of their total wealth without being subject to the genera-tion-skipping tax.

What if you need the money you gave away? Can you get it back? Will it be subject to gift taxes? Will the money be there or will most of it be spent or lost through a divorce? Who knows? So be cautious when using a giving strategy.

# Everything is Yours
(Including the Life Insurance)

It is not uncommon for a Will to direct everything to be transferred upon death to the surviving spouse. Especially, since the United States Federal government does not impose an estate or gift tax on the amount transferred to the surviving spouse as long as he/she is an United States Citizen. There is a limit to the amount transferable to a spouse who is not a United States Citizen.

The problem with transferring everything to the surviving spouse is the deceased individual does not get to utilize his/her Unified Estate Tax Credit. That is not a problem if your taxable estate is under $1,500,000. As of 2004, because of the Unified Estate Tax Credit, $1,500,000 can transfer estate tax-free to a nonspouse (children, friends, etc.). If a married person has a taxable estate valued over $1,500,000, they may want a trust to inherit part of their assets. The trust can be designed to take advantage of the deceased person's Unified Estate Tax Credit and provide income for the surviving spouse.

What is a trust? A trust is a legal contract that can own assets for the benefit of another. In the contract you specify who will oversee the trust assets and how the money is to be managed. When you give assets to the trust, then legally the trust owns it not you. In some cases, you can be the trustee. It is similar to leasing a car. You are not the owner of the car. However, you can use it. There are two main types of trusts: revocable and irrevocable. Revocable means you can change your mind; you can revocalize your will. Since you can change your mind, you run the risk of the assets being included in your estate. To permanently direct assets out of your estate you can use an irrevocable trust. Irrevocable means you cannot change your mind. Once completed, it cannot be changed. It is irreversible! That is why it is important to have an experienced, competent estate tax attorney working with you.

As of 2004, upon the death of the surviving spouse, a taxable estate worth over $3 million will have up to 9 months to pay $704,200 in estate taxes. What if the estate consists mainly of assets that are not quick to sell or recently devalued? How will the estate pay the tax?

Life insurance is a great way to provide cash to your estate. However, you have to be careful how it is owned, or you will run the risk of the death benefit proceeds being subject to estate taxes. Life insurance can be owned by an irrevocable trust, and if properly structured, the estate can avoid the cost of paying estate taxes on the life insurance death benefit proceeds.

# Have Trust

Once again, the main disadvantage of giving everything to your spouse is that your Unified Estate Tax Credit is not fully utilized (refer to the Unified Estate Tax Credit Equivalent Schedule listed below). Due to the credit, each individual has a maximum he/she can give away or transfer upon death without having to pay an estate tax. By using an irrevocable trust you can utilize your individual estate tax credit.

For example, a husband with an estate worth $3 million dies in year 2004. $1.5 million of his estate transfers into an irrevocable trust for the benefit of his two children, thus utilizing the husband's estate tax credit. His wife receives the income from the trust with very restricted access to the trust's principle. These trust assets are no longer included in her estate. The balance of the husband's estate ($1.5 million) passes to his wife. Eventually his wife passes away in 2005, another $1,500,000 can be transferred to the children, free of estate taxes, thus utilizing the wife's estate tax credit. By using this strategy, $3 million dollars was transferred free of estate taxes to the children.

**Unified Estate Tax Credit**
**Equivalent Schedule** (as of year 2004)

| Year | Equivalent Estate |
| --- | --- |
| 2002–2003 | $1,000,000 |
| 2004–2005 | $1,500,000 |
| 2006–2008 | $2,000,000 |
| 2009 | $3,500,000 |
| 2010 | N/A |
| 2011 | $1,000,000 |

# Family Business

Have you ever thought about converting your "estate" into a "family business"? You can establish a family limited partnership and have your assets owned by the partnership. You can issue two types of ownership: general partner (controls assets) and limited partner (does not control assets). You may want to be the general partner and have your family as limited partners. Since limited partners lack control, their ownership in the partnership is often valued at a discount. If properly structured, you are able to reduce your estate while maintaining certain control over the assets. The end result is tax savings and a method of transferring your estate without giving up complete control.

What if you already have a business? Who will run the business? Who should inherit the business? What is the value of the business? If your partner dies, who will inherit his/her ownership in the company?

To prevent any unwanted new shareholders or a new ownership structure, a contract called a "buy-sell agreement" can be established. The agreement states that if your partner dies or becomes disabled, you agree to buy out your partner's ownership in the business at a set price or method to determine the price. You never know when a business partner will die or become disabled. Therefore, you need to have enough life insurance, disability insurance, and investments to fund the agreement when needed.

There are special tax breaks for closely held businesses in which the company represents more than 35% of the deceased's adjusted gross estate. The estate tax can be deferred and paid through the government's installment plan (refer to section 6166). A qualifying closely held corporation can buy back stock from the deceased estate without the risk of the distribution being considered as a dividend as long as the distribution is used to cover the cost for the funeral, estate taxes, and administration expenses of the estate (refer to Section 303 Stock Redemption).

Because farm and ranch properties can be worth more if converted to residential land, the government allows working farms and ranches to be valued by their use, instead of the best price for the real estate (refer to Section 2032A Special Use Valuation). This could save the farmer or rancher's heirs a tremendous amount of money. For more information on these US tax codes (Section 6166, Section 303, and Section 2032A) go to:

www.fourmilab.ch/ustax
and/or
www.irs.gov

# Other Strategies

After you die, your spouse may remarry and endanger your children's future inheritance. To solve this problem, you can set up a marital trust that pays an income to the surviving spouse. Once the surviving spouse dies, the principle will transfer to your children and never go to the new spouse.

You could use a charitable remainder trust to reduce your estate and capital gain taxes and produce an income. For example, you own an asset bought for $100,000 that is currently valued at $1,000,000. If you sell it, you could have a significant capital gain tax. To be tax efficient and accomplish your charitable and income goals, place the asset into a charitable remainder trust for the benefit of a tax-qualified church, school, charity, etc. In turn, the trustee can sell your asset tax-free and invest the proceeds into diversified investments that produce a safe income for you. When you die, the income stops and the trust assets transfer to the charity for its use. The asset is out of your estate. You can use part of your charitable remainder trust's income to purchase a $1,000,000 life insurance policy owned by an irrevocable trust for the benefit of your children and to provide an income to your spouse upon your death. It should be structured so that the life insurance death benefit proceeds will not be included in your estate.

There are some estate tax reduction strategies that involve helping individuals save for college. These strategies can help eliminate some of your estate tax and income tax challenges. For more information visit this websites:

www.collegesavings.org/planning/general.htm

www.collegeboard.com/article/0,3868,6-29-0-395,00.html

# INSURE AGAINST THE BUMPS OF LIFE

"The prudent see danger and take refuge but the simple keep going and suffer for it" (Proverbs 22:3, NIV).

Some people have a wrong perspective on insurance. They think of it as a cost. In reality, it is a program of helping other people and yourself. You are donating money to others who are in need and to those who help make the system work. One of the earliest examples of the insurance concept can be found in the Bible:

> "All the believers were together and had everything in common. Selling their possessions and goods, they gave to anyone as he had need. Everyday they continued to meet together in the temple courts. They broke bread in their homes and ate together with glad and sincere hearts..." (Acts 2:44-46, NIV).

> "At the present time your plenty will supply what they need, so that in turn their plenty will supply what you need. Then there will be equality, as it is written: 'He who gathered much did not have too much, and he who gathered little did not have too little'" (2 Corinthians 8:14-15, NIV).

You give a small amount of money to the insurance company so it can contribute to others or yourself whenever the need arises. Even if you never use your insurance, you still bought something. You bought peace of mind and the ability to help someone make it through a disastrous time. Try to look at insurance from this perspective. It will help make the insurance payments less painful.

"The prudent see danger and take refuge but the simple keep going and suffer for it" (Proverbs 22:3, NIV). Insurance is a critical part of protecting your assets and income. The prudent see danger and take refuge by saving money and purchasing whatever insurance is needed for their particular situation. The "simple" are the people who don't want to deal with it. They keep on going and eventually suffer for it. An entire lifetime of savings could easily be wiped out by one accident, sickness, disability, death or lawsuit.

In 2004 the average daily stay in a hospital is $4,416 (The ICA Guide). Ouch! That is why it is important to always have health insurance coverage because you never know when you might need it or become uninsurable and not be able to purchase health insurance.

A twenty year old worker has a 3 in 10 (30%) chance of becoming disabled before reaching retirement age (Disability Benefits SSA Publication No. 05-10029, January 2005). One of every two foreclosures is due to a disability and 64% of all disabilities are not work-related and fall outside the scope of Workers' Compensation (National Safety Council, *Accident Facts*). According to the Social Security Handbook, roughly 70% of all Social Security disability applicants are rejected. If you become permanently disabled, do you have enough insurance and investments to provide a lifetime of income? If you do not, then you need to obtain disability insurance coverage. Most disability plans pay 60% to 70% of your current salary. If your company or you pay for your disability insurance with pretax dollars (meaning the money has not been taxed yet), then your disability income benefit will be taxable when paid to you. That is why most chose to pay with after-tax dollars so that their disability benefit will be tax-free when paid to them.

According to a study in the New England Journal of Medicine, it is estimated that 43% of those over age 65 will be in a nursing home sometime during their lives. The average annual cost of nursing home care is more than $57,000 (Mature Market Institute 2003), and in some parts of the country exceeds $100,000. That is now; so, imagine what it is going to be in the future. Are you financially prepared to cover this cost? Are your parents prepared? You both may need long-term care insurance.

Make sure that the property insurance coverage you have protects you from the devastating financial results of theft, vandalism, fire, earthquake, flood, hurricane, and other disasters. You may need insurance coverage to help pay claims if someone gets hurt on or by your property (real estate, car, boat, etc.) or by the advice and service you provide.

Sadly, we live in a world where people sue over almost anything or get divorced over the small things. Did you know that you are nearly three times more likely to be in court than to be hospitalized according to the National Center for State Courts and the American Hospital Association (1999). You may win a major lawsuit against you, but do you have the $15,000 to $30,000 to pay your lawyer? Do you have a team of lawyers you can call anytime and get certain legal advice without worrying about getting a bill? There are companies like Pre-Paid Legal Services®, Inc. that offer their members an affordable way to receive free or discounted legal services for Will preparation and updates, motor vehicle violations, trial defense, IRS audit, Trust preparation, etc. For more information on Pre-Paid Legal Services®, Inc. visit their website:

www.prepaidlegal.com

# Life Insurance

You can save a tremendous amount of money over the long run by purchasing the correct amount and type of insurance for your needs. There are two main types of life insurance: term insurance and permanent insurance. Term insurance is designed to cover you for a duration of time (5, 10, 15, 20, 30 years). Permanent insurance is designed to cover you for your entire life. Which is better?

**The answer is both. Each one of them serves a different need.**

Permanent insurance usually works best for cash accumulation and paying for burial expenses, taxes associated with death, and any other permanent needs. Term insurance often works best for covering needs that will cease before the term ends, such as paying for college, paying off a mortgage, and other debts.

Think about it. Let's say you purchase a level 20 year term life insurance policy. That means for the next 20 years the insurance company cannot increase the price they are charging you for the amount of coverage you purchased. Twenty years from now, God be willing, you will have enough money set aside for retirement, your children's college education, and you are debt free. Thus, you may not need life insurance coverage anymore. Some policies will also let you convert into a permanent insurance policy.

Obviously, the older you get, the higher the risk you will die; thus, the higher the cost to insure you. Eventually, the cost may be too high to afford. To keep the payment level, the insurance company requires you to overpay in the early years to cover the future cost of the policy. With permanent policies the overpayment goes into a savings account called cash value. The savings account receives a tax-favored status.

Generally, permanent insurance has a cash value and term does not. As a result, permanent insurance in the short run is more expensive than term insurance. Remember, for permanent needs use permanent insurance, and for temporary needs use term insurance. Some life insurance products have living benefits that pay part of the death benefit while the insured is living and the other part when the insured dies. To receive the living benefit there has to be a qualifying event like a terminal illness or long-term care need. If you become terminally ill or need long-term care this type of living benefit can help you pay the bills and allow you time to spend with your family before you die. Almost half of all Americans now turning age 65 will be admitted to a nursing home at some time in their lives (Wall Street Journal, 2004).

# Life Insurance Worksheet

To find out how much coverage you need, total up the costs of your needs (TOTAL NEED) and subtract them from your current coverage (TOTAL COVERAGE).

If my spouse or I died today, I would want to make sure....

☐ My family would receive a yearly income of $_____ for _____ years (for an estimate, take the yearly income amount and times it by the number of years). This does not factor in inflation or interest made from investing your life insurance proceeds.

☐ Funeral and administration costs and estate taxes are paid.
$_____

☐ All medical bills from the accident or illness will be paid.
$_____

☐ The children's college education will be fully funded.
$_____

☐ Our family will be debt free (mortgage, credit cards, etc.).
$_____

TOTAL NEED: $_____

☐ Social Security & Pension (for an estimate, take the yearly $_____ income amount and times it by the number of years you will receive the income).

☐ Current life insurance coverage $_____
☐ Other assets $_____

TOTAL COVERAGE: $_____

TOTAL NEED MINUS TOTAL COVERAGE: $_____

To get an estimate of your Social Security survivor benefit visit the Social Security Administration website:

www.ssa.gov/pubs/deathbenefits.htm or call 800-772-1213.

Another way to determine your life insurance needs using an internet calculator visit this website:

www.calcbuilder.com/cgi-bin/calcs/INS1.cgi/Kiplinger

Sometimes people say they cannot afford insurance. In reality, they cannot afford to be without it. One medical bill can wipe out a lifetime of savings.

You can make insurance coverage more affordable by self insuring some of the risk. Let's face it—you don't need a lot of "bells and whistles." Insurance is designed primarily to protect you from financial disasters. So, remove the bells and whistles that you do not need and place the savings into a savings account.

Why do you need to pay extra to have a $20 doctor's co-pay plan on your health insurance policy? Why not increase the waiting period on your disability policy? Instead of a 60-day waiting period, have a 90-day waiting period. Why not self-insure yourself by increasing your deductible from $500 to $1,000?

There is a wide variety of insurance coverage out there. It is important to make sure that you have the insurance coverage that is appropriate for you. The problem for many is that they do not know what they need. This is why it is important to work with a trustworthy insurance advisor or CERTIFIED FINANCIAL PLANNER™ professional in order to determine your needs and make a personal insurance plan for you.

# What types of insurance coverage do you need?

☐ Health Insurance

☐ Disability Insurance

☐ Long-term Care Insurance

☐ Life Insurance

☐ Property Insurance (Car, House, Boat, etc.)

☐ _____

☐ _____

☐ _____

☐ _____

# STRATEGY # 3:
## Eliminate High
## Interest Rate Debt

# PERSONAL NOTES

## Strategy #3: Eliminate High Interest Rate Debt

Traps
- Late Fees
- Minimum Payments
- Convenience Checks/Cash Advances
- Unused Credit Cards
- Jointly Owned Credit Cards
- Attention to Interest Rate

Tips
- Stolen cards
- Financial records
- Review Statements
- Rate, Fee, and Other Cost Information Box

Debt
- Money Saved
- Plan
- Overspending
- Create Wealth

Credit Report/Score
- Monitor/Bureaus
- Improve Score

# DEBT TRAPS AND TIPS

"The rich rule over the poor, and the borrower is servant to the lender"
(Proverbs 22:7, NIV).

## Credit Card Traps

**• Late fees**
Not only will the credit card company charge you a late fee (usually $20 to $30); many times they increase your interest rate.

**• Minimum payments**
According to the Federal Reserve's 2001 statistics on consumer debt, the typical credit card holder in America has over an $8,000 balance with an interest rate of 18.9%. For most credit cards, if you only made the minimum payment, it will take more than a quarter of a century to pay off.

**• Convenience checks/cash advances**
In most cases, once you use them, the interest rate charges begin immediately at a higher interest rate and there is a user's fee.

**• Great offers from other credit card companies**
Many of the "great offers" you receive initially tease you with a low interest rate, but after a few months they increase their rate. When you receive an enticing credit card offer, call your current credit card company and ask them to match the offer.

**• Forgetting to cancel unused credit cards**
You may not have debt on your unused credit cards, yet that credit is available to be used anytime. Thus, it can limit the amount you can borrow

when applying for new credit from other institutions. Having a long credit history with one credit card company looks good on your credit report. If you need to get rid of some unused credit cards, start with the newer ones first.

### • Forgetting to cancel jointly owned credit cards
You are responsible for the repayment of anything charged on a jointly owned credit card, even if you never used the card and no longer are associated with that person.

### • Not paying attention to the interest rate
Watch out! Even if the credit card company says that the rate is fixed, it may not be. With some credit card companies, if you are late or underpaid them, that is all the excuse they need to drastically increase your interest rate charge. The credit card company can try to sell your account to another credit card company. Sure, they send you a small notice and a deadline to respond to them. If you do not reject their offer by the deadline, then they can transfer your balance to a new credit card company with a higher interest rate and fees.

# Credit and Debit Card Tips

"Be sure you know the condition of your flocks, give careful attention to your herds; for riches do not endure forever" (Prov. 27:23-24, NIV).

• Write down all of your credit card and debit card phone numbers. Do not include your account numbers. Keep them in a safe place in case your cards are stolen or lost. Keep the list with you. Program their phone numbers into your mobile phone.

• You need to report your stolen cards immediately to limit your liability. If you wait too long, your liability can be unlimited depending on your resident state laws and the credit card company's guidelines.

• Keep all financial records (canceled checks, bank statements, credit card statements, bills, etc.) for at least six years. You may need to keep your brokerage account statements even longer for tax purposes (cost basis).

• Look over your statements for mistakes as soon as they arrive. It is not the consumer's responsibility to prove the billing error. It is the credit card company's responsibility. However, if you find an error, inform your credit card company immediately by:

(1) Calling and reporting the problem. Remember to obtain the proper address of the department that handles billing investigations.

(2) Sending a letter to your card company stating the error. Include your name, address, account number, date, and full description of the error. Send the letter by Certified Mail with a return receipt.

What credit card traps and tips do you need to be concerned about?
When you receive a credit card offer that entices you, make sure you review the *"Rate, Fee, and Other Cost Information Box."* In this sample of a

*"Rate, Fee, and Other Cost Information Box,"* can you spot some of the traps on this advertised 0% rate credit card?

| RATE, FEE AND OTHER COST INFORMATION | | What to look out for… |
|---|---|---|
| Annual Percentage Rate (APR) for Purchases (purchase include balance transfers) | A 0% fixed APR until the first 90th day of the billing cycle. After that, 9.9% fixed. | **Starts out with a low introductory rate, then increases** |
| Other APRS | Cash Advance APR: 19.99% variable. Late Payment APR: Late twice during a six month period: 19.99% fixed on all balances. | **Cash Advance 19.99% "Ouch!" Watch out for the variable rate and the late payment fees** |
| Variable rate information | The cash advance APR varies monthly. It equals the Prime Rate plus 16% for cash advances, but not less than 19.99%. | **Cash advances are expensive on this card** |
| Annual Fee | $30 | **Some cards do not have an Annual Fee** |
| Minimum finance charge | $10 | **The minimum finance charge on small balances can be greater than the interest they charge** |

| Transaction fee for certain purchases | Purchase of wire transfers or money orders or convenience checks: 3% of the amount of each purchase or check, but not less than $5 nor more than $50. | **Those convenience check fees can add up** |
|---|---|---|
| Transaction fee for balance transfers | 3% of the amount of each balance transfer; but not less than $5 nor more than $50. | **The transfer better be worth the fee** |
| Transaction fees for cash advances | All cash advances: 2% of the amount of the advance, but not less than $10. | **More fees for cash advances** |
| Other fees | Late Payment Fee: $29 Over-the-Credit-Limit Fee: $29 | **Watch out for these fees** |

# Money Saved is Money Earned

Money saved is money earned tax-free. Example: You have $5,000. You could put it into an investment earning 8%* or pay off your debt that is charging you 18% interest. If you invest, once you subtract the money lost to debt, your real net rate of return on your money is negative ten percent (8%-18%). What is worse, you still have to pay taxes on your investment's interest. Clearly the best route in this case is to PAY OFF THE DEBT.

An exception to this rule is when your company's retirement plan matches every dollar you invest. A company match is like getting an immediate 100% rate of return on your money! Another exception is when you are trying to build up your emergency fund.

The Bible teaches "...if you lack the means to pay, your very bed will be snatched from under you" (Prov. 22:7,27, NIV). The principle is, in most cases; never borrow money unless you have the means to repay. If you borrow, buy assets that appreciate, then you potentially have a means to repay. If necessary, you can sell the asset, hopefully for a value greater than what you paid for it. In some cases, you can save money by borrowing money to purchase an appreciating asset that you absolutely need! Example: Let's say you are saving $5,000 per year and the house you want to buy is going up $10,000 or more per year, then you will never be able to save enough to pay cash for the house. In this example, you should borrow the money in the form of a mortgage and use the $5,000 per year to pay off the mortgage.*

With almost everything you purchase, its value fluctuates. This is why mortgage companies require you to make a 20% down payment on your house to avoid paying PMI (the insurance that protects your lender in case you default on the loan). If you need a house to live in for at least 3 or more years and you can afford the house payments, taxes, and mainte-nance, then look into purchasing a house. Sometimes it is better to borrow than to save, if the amount you are able to save is not keeping up with the appreciation on the house you want to buy.

Purchasing a house is something you enter into with a lot of prayer and God's direction. It is a long term commitment that can financially hurt you because house prices can decrease, your job can be lost, and job relocation can occur. Besides the mortgage payments, there are taxes and fees associated with buying, selling, and maintaining a house.

*\*This is a hypothetical illustration and is not intended to reflect the actual performance of any particular investment.*

# A Plan to Become Debt Free

Do you really need a new car, house, dress, suit, etc.? The more you own, the more it owns you. The more things you own, the more repairs, up-keep and time that is required. Before you go into debt, you need to ask God if it is truly His will for you to borrow money at this time.

"Now listen, you who say, 'Today or tomorrow we will…carry on business and make money.' Why, you do not even know what will happen tomor-row…Instead, you ought to say, 'If it is the Lord's will, we will…do this…'" (James 4:13-15, NIV).

To become debt free you need a plan. As a general rule, always…

(1)…pay off loans from friends and family members first, regard-less of the interest rate they are charging you. Relationships can easily be damaged over financial loans.

(2) Secondly, pay off the very small debts ($100, $50, etc.). There is great joy in seeing a debt paid off. Plus, on a percentage basis, the minimum finance charges on a small debt balance can be very high. It is important to note that after you pay off a credit card or line of credit do not close that account unless it is a fairly new account. Old established accounts can help improve your credit score.

(3) The next step is to pay off the debt with the highest interest rate, then the next highest rate, then the next highest rate, until you are completely debt free.

You can consolidate all high interest rate debts into one low interest rate debt. Transfer all your credit card balances to the credit card that has the lowest fixed rate. If mortgage rates are low, then consolidate all your debts by refinancing your house. This is a high-risk strategy because you could end up financing that debt over the life of the mortgage and if you have not cured the habit of overspending you end up deeper in debt. Sometimes the best solution is to reduce your spending and find a second job to pay the debt off as soon as possible.

To help you in your planning process you may want to visit CNN money's website:

cgi.money.cnn.com/tools

and look for the Debt Reduction Planner calculator. It allows you to list the different credit cards you have; input their balances, interest rates, and their minimum monthly payments. You can choose a strategy and figure out how you can be debt free in a certain amount of time.

# Curing the Overspending

Why do people overspend?

Is it because they do not follow a spending plan or does it go deeper?

Most people are afraid to get real with their financial situation. Their debt reveals they are not making enough to support their spending habits, yet they do nothing about it. They are afraid to get real because they will have to be responsible with what they learn and earn.

We think the biggest problem with most is their "I deserve" attitude. They say to themselves, "I work hard every week for the money I make. I deserve the newest cars, fashions, products, and services. Even though I cannot afford it, I can still charge it and pay it later." The problem is, when do you plan to repay the debt? Is it next week, next year, next decade or never?

The Bible teaches in Proverbs 37:21-24, NIV: "The wicked borrow and do not repay, but the righteous give generously; those the LORD blesses will inherit the land, but those he curses will be cut off. If the LORD delights in a man's way, he makes his steps firm; though he stumble, he will not fall, for the LORD upholds him with his hand."

On average, Americans spend more than they make and save very little. What a dangerous combination. After a while they have to refinance their house to pay off their credit card debts. Then a few years later they have to do it all over.

The Bible warns, "Anyone, then, who knows the good he ought to do and doesn't do it, sins…weep and wail because of the misery that is coming upon you…You have lived on earth in luxury and self-indulgence. You have fattened yourselves in the day of slaughter" (James 4:14-5:5).

Are you living a life based on self-indulgence or are you living a life based on God honoring principles?

What do you need to do to stop overspending?

# Eliminate Debt and Protect Your Credit Rating

Only 4% to 5% of all Americans will retire financially independent. Many are drowning in a sea of high interest rate debt. They need a plan and solution to get them out of debt. This is why there are companies like EverydayWealth that provide a personalized step-by-step guide to become debt free faster, monitor credit, and create wealth.

There is a cornucopia of information and tools, live telecourses with financial experts, and "Ask An Expert" to make better financial decisions. Monthly, subscribers receive their updated credit report to monitor their credit, identify fraudulent activity, and use the necessary tools to maintain or improve their credit rating. Almost everyone needs to monitor their credit. Even if they never borrow money, their credit rating may affect their insurance rates, future employment, and their ability to rent certain items.

One in 20 Americans becomes a victim of credit fraud, and one in 50 becomes a victim of identity theft. It can be a real nightmare to untangle. The primary issue with credit fraud is not the charges, but the damage that is done to your credit rating. While you are usually only responsible for up to $50 of the charges, the real cost comes with the hassle of repairing the fraud and the time spent clearing your name. By simply reviewing your credit report each month, you can help protect yourself.

**Identity Theft**—While there is no way to prevent it completely, if you can detect it early, you can stop it before the damage becomes severe. By simply reviewing your credit report and statements monthly, you can detect unauthorized activity and suspicious new accounts or charges before it impacts your credit. It brings peace of mind knowing you can help prevent thieves from causing serious credit damage to you.

**Inaccuracies and Errors**—Inaccuracies and errors occur often and can hurt you from borrowing, and getting the best interest and insurance rates. By keeping track of your credit over time, you can recognize times when you may be eligible for better rates. Even a small savings on interest means more money in your future. What are you doing to protect your credit rating?

How are you planning to eliminate your debt and protect your credit rating? I encourage you to purchase the EverydayWealth system or a system like it to monitor your credit. For more information on EverydayWealth visit this website:

www.wealthlink.com/planner

# A Grown-Up's Report Card

"A good name is more desirable than great riches" (Prov. 22:1, NIV).

Your credit report is your financial report card that reveals what kind of financial steward you are to lenders and future employers. Maintaining a good financial reputation is a top priority. Before you borrow a large sum of money, it is important to ask, "What are the major credit bureaus saying about me?" For a fee, each credit bureau will send you your credit report. Once you receive it, look for mistakes. If you find one, fill out a "request for reinvestigation" form to have the mistake corrected. If you find anything that may be misinterpreted, you can add an explanation to your credit report (up to 100 words). This is a good way to make sure no one is using your good name and destroying your credit with misinformation. The three major credit bureaus are:

**Equifax**
P.O. Box 740241 Atlanta, GA 30374-0241
(800) 685-1111/www.equifax.com/consumer/consumer.html

**Trans Union Corporation** (Consumer Disclosure Center)
P.O. Box 403 Springfield, PA 19064-0390
(800) 888-4213 (to order a credit report)
(800) 916-8800 (to ask questions concerning your credit report)
www.tuc.com

**Experian**
P.O. Box 2104 Allen, TX 75013-2104
(888) EXPERIAN/www.experian.com

Each year, make sure you go to www.annualcreditreport.com to receive your free annual copy of your credit reports.

# Improving Your Credit Score

If you have a bad credit reputation, it is time to clean it up! A bad credit report can hinder you from opening a checking account, borrowing for a house or car, renting a home, obtaining insurance, and receiving utility services. Many insurance companies use your credit rating to determine what rate to charge you. Certain employers may require a good credit report before they will hire you. Since people cannot see our hearts, they judge us based on how we look, talk, write, and how we manage our money.

When you apply for a loan, most lenders look at your credit score and credit report to determine if they should loan you the money and what rate should they charge you.

Your FICO credit score is determined by five credit data categories. Some are more important than others:

| Percentage of Importance | Credit Data Category |
| --- | --- |
| 35% | Payment History |
| 30% | Amounts Owed |
| 15% | Length of Credit History |
| 10% | New Credit |
| 10% | Types of Credit Used |

Here are some simple ways to help improve your credit rating:

☐ **Improve payment history:** Your payment history is one of the most important parts of your score, so pay your bills on time and repair your credit by using credit wisely! Borrow small amounts of money and over time pay it back to show you can be reliable, responsible, and trustworthy. "Whoever can be trusted with very little can also be trusted with much, and whoever is dishonest with very little will also be dishonest with much" (Luke 16:10, NIV).

Of course, never borrow unless you can pay the money back and you have changed the behaviors that initially
put you into debt.

☐ **Paying off debts or increase credit limit:** The amounts you owe on your debts are almost equally important as your payment history. Paying off debts can help improve your credit score. However, you need to be smart on what you pay off. One of the factors that hurt your credit score is the amount you owe on a credit card as compared to the credit card's limit. The amount you owe on revolving credit (credit cards, lines of credit, etc.) needs to be less than 50% of the revolving credit's limit. If not then you need to increase your credit limit so that it is at least double the amount you owe or pay it down or transfer part of it to other debts so that your balance is below 50% of the credit limit. For example, if you owe $8,000 on a credit card then the credit limit should be at least $16,000 or higher ($8,000 multiplied by 2).

☐ **Keep old credit cards alive:** They look at how long the account has been opened and the activity on the account. As a general rule: the older the account the better.

☐ **Applying for a loan:** Too many recent credit inquiries and too many recently opened credit accounts can hurt your credit score.

☐ **Show job stability.** Prove that you can keep a job and make the payments.

☐ You can use programs like the EverydayWealth system to monitor your progress.

To learn more about the FICO credit scoring visit this website:

www.myfico.com/CreditEducation

If you are in a very desperate situation, you may want to contact:

Consumer Credit Counseling Service (CCCS)
800-251-2227
www.cccsatl.org

CCCS is a nonprofit service that has been around for over three decades. As of January 2004, there was no charge to you for their services. They can help you get your debts under control. They can create a budget and payment plan for you. Most importantly, they can give you hope. CCCS does not report you to the credit bureaus. However, if CCCS negotiates with your creditors, this could affect your credit report. It all depends on how your creditors report the negotiations to the credit bureaus.

# STRATEGY # 4:
## Accumulate
## for Goals

# PERSONAL NOTES

## Strategy #4: Accumulate for Goals

Investing
- Investment Calculator
- Road Blocks
- Inflation
- Compounding
- Loaners
- Owners
- Diversification
- Goals

Income Taxes
- Bible Commands
- Deductions
- Calculations
- Real Take Home
- Capital Gains

Tax-Advantaged College Savings
- Future Cost of College
- Prepay Tuition
- Roth IRA
- Coverdell Education Savings Account
- Custodial Minor's Account (UGMA/UTMA)
- Savings Bonds & I-Bonds

Tax-Advantaged Retirement Savings
- Planning
- Roth IRA
- Traditional IRA
- Annuity
- Cash-Value Life
- Company Sponsored Retirement Plans
- Warning

The Best Investment
- Eternal Plan
- The Most Important Relationship
- Only One
- Creation
- Developing a Relationship
- Commit

# INVEST FOR THE FUTURE

"...he who gathers money little by little makes it grow"
(Proverbs 13:11, NIV).

## Investment Calculators

### (1) $100 Per Month Investment*

| Rate | 5 Years | 10 Years | 15 Years | 20 Years | 25 Years | 30 Years | 35 Years | 40 Years |
|---|---|---|---|---|---|---|---|---|
| 3% | $6,465 | $13,974 | $22,697 | $32,830 | $44,601 | $58,274 | $74,156 | $32,620 |
| 4% | $6,630 | $14,725 | $24,609 | $36,677 | $51,413 | $69,405 | $91,373 | $48,010 |
| 5% | $6,801 | $15,528 | $26,729 | $41,103 | $59,551 | $83,226 | $113,609 | $70,400 |
| 6% | $6,977 | $16,388 | $29,082 | $46,204 | $69,299 | $100,452 | $142,471 | $102,857 |
| 7% | $7,159 | $17,308 | $31,696 | $52,093 | $81,007 | $121,997 | $180,105 | $149,745 |
| 8% | $7,348 | $18,295 | $34,604 | $58,902 | $95,103 | $149,036 | $229,388 | $217,245 |
| 9% | $7,542 | $19,351 | $37,841 | $66,789 | $112,112 | $183,074 | $294,178 | $314,094 |
| 10% | $7,744 | $20,484 | $41,447 | $75,937 | $132,683 | $226,049 | $379,664 | $452,593 |
| 11% | $7,952 | $21,700 | $45,469 | $86,564 | $157,613 | $280,452 | $492,830 | $650,009 |
| 12% | $8,167 | $23,004 | $49,958 | $98,926 | $187,885 | $349,496 | $643,096 | $930,510 |

### (2) $10,000 Lump Sum Investment*

| Rate | 5 Years | 10 Years | 15 Years | 20 Years | 25 Years | 30 Years | 35 Years | 40 Years |
|---|---|---|---|---|---|---|---|---|
| 3% | $11,593 | $13,439 | $15,580 | $18,061 | $20,938 | $24,273 | $28,139 | $32,620 |
| 4% | $12,167 | $14,802 | $18,009 | $21,911 | $26,658 | $32,434 | $39,461 | $48,010 |
| 5% | $12,763 | $16,289 | $20,789 | $26,533 | $33,864 | $43,219 | $55,160 | $70,400 |
| 6% | $13,382 | $17,908 | $23,966 | $32,071 | $42,919 | $57,435 | $76,861 | $102,857 |
| 7% | $14,026 | $19,672 | $27,590 | $38,697 | $54,274 | $76,123 | $106,766 | $149,745 |
| 8% | $14,693 | $21,589 | $31,722 | $46,610 | $68,485 | $100,627 | $147,853 | $217,245 |
| 9% | $15,386 | $23,674 | $36,425 | $56,044 | $86,231 | $132,677 | $204,140 | $314,094 |
| 10% | $16,105 | $25,937 | $41,772 | $67,275 | $108,347 | $174,494 | $281,024 | $452,593 |
| 11% | $16,851 | $28,394 | $47,846 | $80,623 | $135,855 | $228,923 | $385,749 | $650,009 |
| 12% | $17,623 | $31,058 | $54,736 | $96,463 | $170,001 | $299,599 | $527,996 | $930,510 |

### (3) Annual Investment Required to Reach $100,000*

| Rate | 5 Years | 10 Years | 15 Years | 20 Years | 25 Years | 30 Years | 35 Years | 40 Years |
|---|---|---|---|---|---|---|---|---|
| 3% | $18,287 | $8,469 | $5,220 | $3,613 | $2,663 | $2,041 | $1,606 | $1,288 |
| 4% | $17,753 | $8,009 | $4,802 | $3,229 | $2,309 | $1,714 | $1,306 | $1,012 |
| 5% | $17,236 | $7,572 | $4,414 | $2,880 | $1,995 | $1,433 | $1,054 | $788 |
| 6% | $16,736 | $7,157 | $4,053 | $2,565 | $1,720 | $1,193 | $847 | $610 |
| 7% | $16,251 | $6,764 | $3,719 | $2,280 | $1,478 | $989 | $676 | $468 |
| 8% | $15,783 | $6,392 | $3,410 | $2,023 | $1,267 | $817 | $537 | $357 |
| 9% | $15,330 | $6,039 | $3,125 | $1,793 | $1,083 | $673 | $425 | $272 |
| 10% | $14,891 | $5,704 | $2,861 | $1,587 | $924 | $553 | $335 | $205 |
| 11% | $14,466 | $5,388 | $2,618 | $1,403 | $787 | $453 | $264 | $155 |
| 12% | $14,054 | $5,088 | $2,395 | $1,239 | $670 | $370 | $207 | $116 |

### (4) Lump Sum Required to Reach $100,000*

| Rate | 5 Years | 10 Years | 15 Years | 20 Years | 25 Years | 30 Years | 35 Years | 40 Years |
|---|---|---|---|---|---|---|---|---|
| 3% | $86,261 | $74,409 | $64,186 | $55,368 | $47,761 | $41,199 | $35,538 | $30,656 |
| 4% | $82,193 | $67,556 | $55,526 | $45,639 | $37,512 | $30,832 | $25,342 | $20,829 |
| 5% | $78,353 | $61,391 | $48,102 | $37,689 | $29,530 | $23,138 | $18,129 | $14,205 |
| 6% | $74,726 | $55,839 | $41,727 | $31,180 | $23,300 | $17,411 | $13,011 | $9,722 |
| 7% | $71,299 | $50,835 | $36,245 | $25,842 | $18,425 | $13,137 | $9,366 | $6,678 |
| 8% | $68,058 | $46,319 | $31,524 | $21,455 | $14,602 | $9,938 | $6,763 | $4,603 |
| 9% | $64,993 | $42,241 | $27,454 | $17,843 | $11,597 | $7,537 | $4,899 | $3,184 |
| 10% | $62,092 | $38,554 | $23,939 | $14,864 | $9,230 | $5,731 | $3,558 | $2,209 |
| 11% | $59,345 | $35,218 | $20,900 | $12,403 | $7,361 | $4,368 | $2,592 | $1,538 |
| 12% | $56,743 | $32,197 | $18,270 | $10,367 | $5,882 | $3,338 | $1,894 | $1,075 |

*These are year end values, compounded annually. These charts are for illustration purposes only and do not represent the returns of any type of investment and usually, the higher the return, the higher the risk.

# Road Blocks to Investing

## Yourself

When it comes to investing, most of the time fear and greed dictate the actions of those who lack financial knowledge. "People who want to get rich fall into temptation and a trap and into many foolish and harmful desires that plunge men into ruin and destruction" (1 Timothy 6:9, NIV). Stick to the plan. Do not overreact and allow short-term market fluctuations to tempt you. Chasing "hot" tips can damage your long-term plans. Most people know just enough about investments to make them dangerous. They sell or choose certain investments when they should not. Most should work with a financial advisor. There is a reason the Bible says, "Make plans by seeking advice" (Prov. 20:18, NIV); "Listen to advice and accept instruction, and in the end you will be wise" (Prov. 19:20. NIV); "A wise man listens to advice" (Prov. 12:15, NIV). It is prideful to believe you can be an expert on everything. Being humble and seeking advice is a part of being a servant of God: "Pride goes before destruction" (Prov. 16:18, NIV). "For everyone who exalts himself will be humbled, and he who humbles himself will be exalted" (Luke 14:11 & 18:14, NIV).

## Inflation (the rising cost of living)

Not including inflation in your long-term plans can have devastating effects on your ability to reach your financial goals. Time: If you wait too long, you will miss out on the power of long-term compounding and the opportunity to easily reach your financial goals. Investment: Choosing improper investments for your goals can come at a great cost. Example: $10,000 compounded annually at 4% in 30 years grows to $32,433; at 8% it grows to $174,494*. Which one would you like to have? *This is a hypothetical illustration and is not intended to reflect the actual performance of any particular investment.

## Taxes

Understanding how taxes affect your investments' real rate of return and choosing proper tax-advantaged products can make the difference between achieving or not achieving a financial goal. Plus, it can save you a tremendous amount of money.

### Diversification

"Don't put all your eggs in one basket." Sure you can become rich quickly by picking that one great investment, but you can also get real poor, real quick, by choosing the wrong investment. "Give portions to seven, yes to eight, for you do not know what disaster may come upon the land" (Ecc. 11:2, NIV).

# Inflation

Have you ever heard someone say…
*"I remember when a dime could buy you a soda pop!"*
*"I remember when a penny could buy you a handful of candy!"*
*"I remember when gas prices were less than a dollar per gallon!"*

**Over a twenty year period of time (1980–2004)…**

**The cost of a Single-family home has increased over 193%, from $62,200 to $182,500.***

**The average automobile cost increased over 218%, from $6,200 to $19,685.***

**The average daily stay in the hospital increased over 1,222%, from $344 to $4,416.***

Do your plans factor in the effects of inflation?
The average cost of living usually increases 3% or higher yearly.
$10,000 invested growing at 3% in 15 years grows to $15,580. In other words, if the cost of living increases 3% yearly for the next 15 years then you will need $15,580 to buy what $10,000 buys today! If the average increase is 5% then in 15 years you will need $18,009 to buy what $10,000 buys today. Look at the Investment Calculators at the beginning of this chapter to help you do your own inflation calculation.

Are your investments at least keeping up with the growing cost of living (inflation)?

* The figures shown are past results and are not predictive of future results. Current results may be lower or higher than those shown. The information comes from "The ICA Guide."

# The Power of Compounding

"...he who gathers money little by little makes it grow" (Prov. 13:11, NIV). Compounding occurs when your investment makes a profit; you reinvest the profit into your investment, allowing it to grow bigger and bigger. It is like the snowball effect. You begin with a small snowball and roll it and roll it and as long as there is snow then it gets larger and larger.

Through the power of compounding, your investment can double in value in a short period of time. To obtain an estimate on how many years until your investment will double in value, divide 72 by your interest rate or investment rate of return.

Example: 72/12 = 6, thus a one-time investment growing at 12% should double about every 6 years.

A one-time $5,000 investment 6 years later
approximately grows to $10,000;
6 more years around $20,000;
6 more years around $40,000;
6 more years around $80,000;
6 more years around $160,000;
6 more years around $320,000;
6 more years around $640,000;
6 more years, over a million.

This is just an estimate and
most long-term investments fluctuate in value.*

*This illustrates the value of regular annual investments at the end of each year and reinvesting all the gains and interest the investment makes at the same fixed rate to allow for the compounding effect. This does not reflect an actual return in any particular investment. In some investments, the value of your original investment and the return will vary.

What about investing money every year…

$1,000 Invested Annually at the End of Each Year*

|  | 10 years | 20 years | 30 years | 40 years |
|---|---|---|---|---|
| 4% | $12,006 | $29,778 | $56,084 | $95,025 |
| 8% | $14,486 | $45,761 | $113,283 | $259,056 |
| 12% | $17,546 | $72,052 | $241,332 | $767,091 |

Married couple John and Sue were both age 20 when Sue started investing $2,000 per year into tax-deferred investments. After 10 years, she decided to stop investing and let her money grow until she retired. Her husband John decided to start investing when Sue stopped.

He invested $2,000 a year in tax-deferred investments from the time he was 30 until he retired at age 65. They both earned 8% on their investments.

When they reached age 65, Sue had almost hundred thousand more than John. Even though Sue invested $50,000 less, because she invested early, she made more money through the power of compounding!*

*This illustrates the value of regular annual investments at the end of each year and reinvesting all the gains and interest the investment makes at the same fixed rate to allow for the compounding effect. This does not reflect an actual return in any particular investment. In some investments, the value of your original investment and the return will vary.

# Style of Investing

## Loaner

When it comes to investing, most people are either loaners or owners, or a combination of both. The loaner style of investing requires lending money, charging interest for a profit, and selling the loan to other lenders for a profit. This style of investing gives you set income but not without risk. Here are some examples of the risk of loaning money:

(1)  Loss of Principle: The borrower may not pay you back.

(2)  Inflation: The interest rate does not keep up with the cost of living.

(3)  Interest Rate Risk: For an example, you loan $10,000 paying 8% annual interest rate for 10 years. Five years later you need the money, so you sell it. If new comparable loans pay 10% interest, then no one would want your 8% interest loan unless you sold it to them at a price below what you originally paid for it.

(4)  Credit Quality: If your borrower's risk of defaulting on the loan increases, then your ability to sell their loan and get a return of your principle decreases.

## Owner

The owner style of investing produces a profit mainly by selling an investment for a higher price than what was originally paid for it (capital gains) or the investment produces an income. The way you make money with real estate is very similar to the way you make money with the other types of ownership investing. You buy a house and rent it out (income) and then you sell it hopefully for a profit (capital gain). What if you bought your home as a real estate investment and later that year mortgage rates went up at an alarming rate, the demand for housing dropped drastically, and so did house prices. You thought you bought a great house at a very reasonable price. You paid $250,000 for the house, but now it is only worth $190,000. Do you panic and sell your house? No! You wait because you believe that some day it will be worth more than the $250,000. This is the same way you need to treat any good solid investment. If you purchased it as a long-term investment, then treat it like a long-term investment! If it is selling at a discount, do not sell it. Instead, buy more of it. "He who gathers money little by little makes it grow" (Prov. 13:11, NIV).

Many times greed gets people to buy investments when they are too hot (overpriced), and fear gets them to sell when they are under-priced. They should be buying when they are under-priced (low) and selling when they are overpriced (high). Greed and fear cause most to do the opposite of what they should do. Remember that it takes patience and courage to be a good investor. Is your goal to get rich quick or is it to be a prudent investor? "People who want to get rich fall into temptation and a trap and into many foolish and harmful desires that plunge men into ruin and destruction" (1 Timothy 6:9, NIV).

# Is Investing Gambling

Some people believe that investing is gambling. Just because something has risk does not mean that it is gambling. Everything in life has a risk. The major difference between gambling and investing is that with gambling there is an extremely high probability of loss. Once it is lost, it is lost forever!

As long as the investment does not cease to exist, then there is still an opportunity for it to recover. It may take years until it recovers, but at least there is a possibility. If it was a good buy at $100,000, it may be an even better buy at $80,000. It depends on the investment and how long you can wait.

Jesus taught a parable on the kingdom of God in Matthew 25:1,14-30, NIV: "'Master,' he said, 'you entrusted me with five talents {a talent is worth thousands of dollars}. See, I have gained five more.' His master replied, 'Well-done, good and faithful servant! You have been faithful with a few things; I will put you in charge of many things…' Then the man who had received the one talent came. 'Master,' he said, '…I was afraid and went out and hid your talent in the ground. See, here is what belongs to you.' His master replied, 'You wicked, lazy servant!…you should have put my money on deposit with the bankers, so that when I returned I would have received it back with interest. 'Take the talent from him…and throw that worthless servant outside.'"

Where are the talents in your life?

Are you burying them in your checking account?

Or are you investing them?

And into what types of investments?

"Everything under heaven belongs to God" (Job 41:11, NIV).

God entrusts you with His resources. God wants you to use your resources wisely (time, skills, money), by investing your life into serving Him and others, and by taking prudent risks. Have you ever heard "if you don't use it, you lose it?" This is true with almost everything in life. Over time, if your money is not growing then you are losing money due to your reduction in purchasing power (inflation).

# In Life You Either...

...work for money, have money work for you through investments, hire others to work for you, or do a combination of the above.

One of the ways to invest for your future is by starting your own business and hiring others to work the business with you. Most people work for money and invest; yet, very few have the courage to be a business owner. The tax advantages of owning your own business are numerous. Many of us need more income and tax breaks to reach our financial goals, or we need to lower our current spending. You can build a business by yourself or you can build it with others. However, if you are building it by yourself, you will always be limited by your time and resources. The Bible teaches "Two are better than one, because they have a good return for their work: If one falls down, his friend can help him up. But pity the man who falls and has no one to help him up!" (Ecc. 4:9,10 NIV). If you lost your job or could not work, who is going to pick you up when you fall down? If you are a business owner and you are unable to work, then your employees or business partners can help carry you until you recover or your disability insurance begins.

It takes money to make money and it takes courage to be a business owner. One of the biggest fears with any new business is rejection. My father-in-law taught me this saying: "Some will! Some won't! Who's next!" His point was: do not let rejection stop you from fulfilling God's purpose for you. Think about God's gift of salvation. It is the greatest gift one could ever receive; yet, Jesus said, "[One person] hears the message...and does not understand it, the evil one comes and snatches away what was sown in his heart.... [Another person] hears the word and at once receives it with joy. But since he has no root, he lasts only a short time. When trouble or persecution comes because of the word, he quickly falls away...[Another] hears the word, but the worries of this life and the deceitfulness of wealth choke it, making it unfruitful...[Another] hears the word and understands it. He produces a crop, yielding a hundred, sixty or thirty times what was

sown" (Mat. 13:19-23, NIV). Only a small percentage of seed sowed ever produces a crop. So it is easy to get discouraged when your efforts are rejected. However, you know that if you keep on sowing good seed then eventually your efforts will produce "a crop, yielding a hundred, sixty or thirty times what was sown." The key is keep sowing good seed and having the patience and resources to survive in the beginning stages of your business development. "Let us not become weary in doing good, for at the proper time we will reap a harvest if we do not give up. Therefore, as we have opportunity, let us do good to all people"
(Gal. 6:9,10, NIV).

There are innovative ways out there to build a business. As you explore business opportunities, it is important to know that some businesses are illegal pyramid schemes. By definition a pyramid scheme is an illegal get-rich-quick scheme in which recruited people make payments to others above them in a hierarchy while expecting to receive payments from those recruited below them. In time, they fail to get enough people to sustain the payment structure, and the scheme collapses with the majority losing the money they contributed. The Federal Trade Commission defines pyramid schemes as plans which "concentrate on the commissions you could earn just for recruiting new distributors," and which "generally ignore the marketing and selling of their products and services." If a network marketing company sells a product/service that is extremely overpriced or worthless, then it is probably a pyramid scheme.

There is nothing wrong with being rich. However, the Bible warns "…the love of money is a root of all kinds of evil. Some people, eager for money, have wandered from the faith and pierced themselves with many griefs. But you, man of God, flee from all this, and pursue righteousness, godliness, faith, love, endurance and gentleness….put [your] hope in God, who richly provides us with everything for our enjoyment. Command those who are rich in this present world not to be arrogant nor to put their hope in wealth, which is so uncertain, but to put their hope in God, who richly provides us with everything for our enjoyment. Command them to do good, to be rich in good deeds, and to be generous and willing to share" (1 Tim. 6:9-11; 17-19, NIV).

The major advantage of a legal network marketing company is their compensation structure. It is like a typical corporation structure in which you are a National Sales Manager in charge of hiring Regional Sales people under you to work for the company, who in-turn hire Local Sales people under them, etc. As long as the company has a strong product/service and has enough customers, then the company will survive. It can start with as little as a handful of people who commit to continuously purchase and market the product/service and find a handful of people to make the same commitment. By working as a team, you are able to use your time wisely. The Bible warns, "Do not wear yourself out to get rich; have the wisdom to show restraint" (Prov. 3:24, NIV). Due to the compounding effect of networking, eventually your team should have thousands of people marketing and using the service and generating a significant income for you and many others in your team.

What are you passionate about? I encourage you to market it through your own business.

## Diversify or Insure Your Money

"Give portions to seven, yes to eight, for you do not know what disaster may come upon the land" (Ecc. 11:2, NIV). Look at Tom and Debbie. Tom invested $50,000 into one investment that promised him a 6% annual return. Debbie invested $10,000 into five different investments, totaling $50,000. After twenty-five years Debbie had almost $100,000 more than Tom. However, in one of Debbie's investments she had lost all $10,000. That investment could have been a business that she started that

| After 25 Years | |
| --- | --- |
| Tom | |
| 6% | $214,593 |
| | |
| Debbie | |
| (loss) | $           0 |
| 5% | $  33,863 |
| 7% | $  54,274 |
| 9% | $  86,230 |
| 11% | $135,854 |
| | $310,221 |

went under or a lost piece of collectable jewelry. The point is not what she invested in, but what she did with her investments. She diversified her investments and some of her investments took great courage.

Many times it is our faith and hope that gives us the courage to ride out the storms and focus on the future:

"…fix our eyes not on what is seen, but on what is unseen. For what is seen is temporary…" (2 Cor. 4:18, NIV).

To learn more about investing visit some of our favorite financial web-sites...

www.moneycentral.msn
www.bloomberg.com
finance.yahoo.com
www.investorwords.com
www.morningstar.com
www.marketwatch.com
www.kiplinger.com/basics
www.crown.org/library
money.cnn.com
www.usatoday.com
online.wsj.com

The advice and views expressed from each website listed in this book maybe be different from the views and advice Anissa and Dustin LaPorte would provide. Anissa and Dustin LaPorte cannot guarantee the accuracy of the websites, nor can Anissa and Dustin LaPorte guarantee these web-sites still offer their services.

# INCOME TAXES

"…pay taxes, for the authorities are God's servants, who give their full time to governing" (Romans 13:6, NIV).

Paying taxes is a part of life. Keep in mind that the Bible actually commands us to do so. "Consequently, he who rebels against the authority is rebelling against what God has instituted, and those who do so will bring judgment on themselves…For he is God's servant to do you good. But if you do wrong, be afraid, for

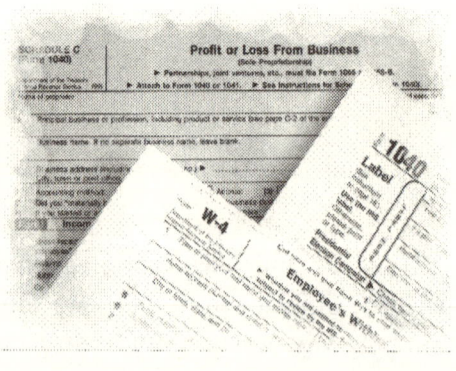

he does not bear the sword for nothing. He is God's servant, an agent of wrath to bring punishment on the wrongdoer. Therefore, it is necessary to submit to the authorities, not only because of possible punishment but also because of conscience. This is also why you pay taxes, for the authorities are God's servants, who give their full time to governing. Give everyone what you owe him: If you owe taxes, pay taxes; if revenue, then revenue; if respect, then respect; if honor, then honor. Let no debt remain outstanding, except the continuing debt to love one another, for he who loves his fellowman has fulfilled the law…." (Rom. 13:2-8, NIV). "Then [Jesus] said to them, 'Give to Caesar what is Caesar's, and to God what is God's'" (Mat. 22:21, NIV).

Our goal is to give you a better understanding of how our income tax system works. In turn, you will have a greater insight on how to maneuver your spending and investing patterns. The more you understand about how the tax system works, the more you will realize how tax-advantaged investments and strategies benefit you and how you can avoid paying more to Caesar (the government) than what is required.

Dustin and Anissa LaPorte are not tax advisors. To understand your personal tax situation completely, always consult your tax advisor. The information provided in this book is based on January 2004 tax laws.

## Income Tax Deductions

Besides providing income to keep our government alive, taxes also serve as a tool to encourage certain behaviors in society. The government wants you to save for retirement and college, give to charities, and buy a house. Thus, they give certain tax breaks. If you do not know they exist, how are you going to take advantage of them? If you know the rules, you can win in the financial game.

Let's take a look at our tax system. For most, because they are alive, they get a tax deduction. There is a personal and dependency exemption that is available for everyone who makes below a certain amount of income and does not have his/her exemption claimed by another.

Personal & Dependency Exemption: $3,100 in the year 2004, this exemption has been phased out for individuals with Adjusted Gross Income starting at $214,050 (Married Couples Filing Jointly or Surviving Spouse), $178,350 (Head of Household), $142,700 (Single), and $107,025 (Married Couples Filing Separately).

Basically, for most U.S. families consisting of a husband, wife, and one young child under age 17, they each receive a $3,100 exemption. Also, they get a choice of a Standard Deduction or Itemized Deduction (mortgage interest, charitable contributions, etc.) whichever is greater. They cannot have both, either one or the other. If they choose the Standard Deduction ($9,700), they can make up to $19,000 without paying Federal income taxes ($9,700+ $3,100 + $3,100 + $3,100).

The Standard Deduction for the year 2004 is $4,850 for a Single person, $7,150 for Head of Household, and $9,700 for a Married person filing jointly. There is an extra deduction if you are blind or age 65 and older: $1,200 for a Single person or Head of Household and $950 for a Married person. The Standard Deduction and many other tax deductions are subtracted from the amount of income you make. However, tax credits are subtracted directly from the amount of taxes you owe.

There are many types of tax credits. For example, as of 2004, there is the Child Tax Credit ($1,000 maximum credit per qualifying child under age 16). The Child Tax Credit goes directly against any Federal taxes you owe. However, the Child Tax Credit is phased out starting at $110,000 for Married filing jointly or surviving spouse, and $75,000 for Single or Head of Household, and $55,000 for Married filing separately.

Let's say a family consisting of a husband, wife, and one child receives $50,300 in income in 2004. Their charitable gifts, mortgage interest on their house, and other Itemized Deductions total $8,000. When comput-

ing their taxes, they will use their Standard Deduction ($9,700 for a married couple filing jointly) because it is greater then their Itemized Deduction ($8,000).

| | |
|---|---|
| **$50,300** | (Total Income) |
| – [**$3,100 X 3**] | (Personal/Dep. Exempt.) |
| – **$ 9,700** | (Standard Deduction) |
| – **$ 1,000** | (401k Contribution) |
| **$20,300** | (Federal Taxable Income) |

Remember they can make $19,000 (Personal & Dependency Exemptions plus Standard Deduction) without paying Federal Income Taxes. For the most part, total income less Personal & Dependency Exemptions less Standard (or Itemized) Deduction less other deductions (Traditional IRA, 401k contributions, etc.) equals the amount subject to Federal income taxes. Under the chart Married Taxpayer Joint and Surviving Spouse, part of their taxable income is taxed at 10% ($0 to $14,300) and another part is taxed at 15% (everything between $14,301 to $58,100). Take the $20,300 taxable income and subtract $14,300 (the first tax bracket), which equals $6,000. $6,000 multiplied by 15% (the next tax bracket) equals $900. [$14,300 X 10%] + [$6,000 X 15%] = the Federal tax due of $2,330. If their child qualifies for the Child Tax Credit, then you can minus $1,000 from the $2,330 (Federal taxes due) for total tax due of $1,330.

This is called a marginal tax system. The more you make, the more they take. This does not include other taxes and fees.

## Married Filing Jointly and Surviving Spouses

| If taxable income is: | Your tax is: |
| --- | --- |
| Not over $14,300 | 10% of taxable income |
| Over $14,300 to $58,100 | $1,430 + 15% of the excess over $14,300 |
| Over $58,100 to $117,250 | $8,000 + 25% of the excess over $58,100 |
| Over $117,250 to $178,650 | $22,787.50 + 28% of the excess over $117,250 |
| Over $178,650 to $319,100 | $39,979.50 + 33% of the excess over $178,650 |
| Over $319,100 | $86,328 + 35% of the excess over $319,100 |

## Single Taxpayers

| If taxable income is: | Your tax is: |
| --- | --- |
| Not over $7,150 | 10% of taxable income |
| Over $7,150 to $29,050 | $715 + 15% of the excess over $7,150 |
| Over $29,050 to $70,350 | $4,000 + 25% of the excess over $29,050 |
| Over $70,350 to $146,750 | $14,325 + 28% of the excess over $70,350 |
| Over $146,750 to $319,100 | $35,717 + 33% of the excess over $146,750 |
| Over $319,100 | $92,592.50 + 35% of the excess over $319,100 |

# What Do You Really Make

Let's say that after state and federal taxes you are able to keep 70% of your total income. The $1,000 you put into your company's 401k retirement account costs you only $700 from your take-home-pay because you saved $300 in taxes. Have in mind, you will still have to pay income taxes when you withdraw the money from your traditional 401k retirement account. In theory, at retirement your income drops; thus, placing you into a lower income tax bracket. If you are going to be in a higher or equal tax bracket when you retire, then you may want to pay the tax now and invest in tax-free investments or accounts.

| | | | Tax Rates | | |
| Yields | 15% | 25% | 28% | 33% | 35% |
|---|---|---|---|---|---|
| 4.00% | 4.71% | 5.33% | 5.56% | 5.97% | 6.00% |
| 4.50% | 5.29% | 6.00% | 6.25% | 6.72% | 6.92% |
| 5.00% | 5.88% | 6.67% | 6.94% | 7.46% | 7.69% |
| 5.50% | 6.47% | 7.33% | 7.64% | 8.21% | 8.46% |
| 6.00% | 7.06% | 8.00% | 8.33% | 8.96% | 9.23% |
| 6.50% | 7.65% | 8.67% | 9.03% | 9.70% | 10.00% |
| 7.00% | 8.24% | 9.33% | 9.72% | 10.45% | 10.77% |
| 7.50% | 8.82% | 10.00% | 10.42% | 11.19% | 11.54% |
| 8.00% | 9.41% | 10.67% | 11.11% | 11.94% | 12.31% |

You can learn a lot from this chart. If you are in the 25% tax bracket then…(1) A tax-free investment that pays 6% is equivalent to a taxable investment that pays 8%. (2) If your taxable investment pays 10% interest, then after taxes it nets 7.5%.

If after Federal and State Taxes you only keep 70% of what you make, you need to make $14,286 to pay off $10,000 on a credit card, car loan, etc. ($10,000 divided by 70% equals $14,286 or $14,286 multiplied by 70% equals $10,000). This does not include what the lender charges you to borrow the money!

# Capital Gains

Have you ever heard the saying, "buy low, sell high"? That type of gain is called a capital gain. That is when you buy an investment at a low price and sell it at a higher price. It is treated differently than the income you receive from your employment or from the interest generated from an investment. Tax laws are constantly changing, but as a general rule, capital gains are usually taxed at an equal or lower rate than ordinary income taxes. The amount you pay in capital gains depends on what ordinary income tax bracket you are in, the type of investment you are selling, and the duration of time you held the investment. If you sell an investment at a lower price than the amount paid for it, this is considered a capital loss. A capital loss can be used to offset capital gains. If your capital losses are greater than part of your capital gains, then your capital losses can be deducted from your ordinary income.

However, there is a limit to how much can be deducted from your ordinary income. Some capital losses can be carried forward to future tax years. You cannot deduct losses from the sale or trade of an investment that result in a wash sale. A wash sale occurs when you sell or trade an investment at a loss and within 30 days before or after acquiring substantially identical investment or a contract/option to buy substantially identical investment. An example of a wash sale is when you sell an investment you own at a loss, then immediately repurchase it.

It is important to keep track of what you paid for an investment, the date of the purchase, and all reinvestments. Knowing this information will help you during tax time and assist you in making tax strategy selling and buying decisions. Plus, never assume that your brokerage firm will keep track of this information for you.

For more information on capital gains refer to IRS Publication 550 called Investment Income and Expenses (Including Capital Gains and Losses). It can be found at the IRS website:

www.irs.gov/pub/irs-pdf/p550.pdf

For the most updated tax information visit:

www.irs.gov

For more information on U.S. tax codes visit:

www.fourmilab.ch/ustax

You can also call the IRS at 800-829-1040.

# TAX-ADVANTAGED COLLEGE SAVINGS

"My people are destroyed from lack of knowledge"
(Hosea 4:6, KJV).

The average annual cost of college (tuition, room, and board) is $28,000 at a private college and $12,000 at a public college (College Board, 2005). It is alarming that tuition costs have increased dramatically over the last 4 years-30% at public colleges and 20% at private colleges (College Board, 2005).

# What four years of college could cost in the future

| Your child's current age | Public school | Private School |
| --- | --- | --- |
| newborn | $172,728 | $368,868 |
| 3 | $145,025 | $309,708 |
| 6 | $121,766 | $260,037 |
| 9 | $102,237 | $218,332 |
| 12 | $85,840 | $183,316 |
| 15 | $72,073 | $153,916 |
| 17 | $64,145 | $136,984 |

\* Source: The College Board for the 2003-2004 school year.
\*\* Assumes college costs increase at 6% a year on average. For illustration only.

Despite the high cost of college tuition, there could be an even higher cost: The cost of not having a college degree. The average person with a B.A. (or higher) will earn over $1,000,000 more in his or her lifetime than a person with only a high school diploma (U.S. Census Bureau, 2003).

# College Savings Ideas

**Prepay Tuition**—If you are confident of the college the person will attend, you may be able to prepay his/her tuition. By prepaying the tuition, you lock in today's tuition costs. Recently, a popular public university raised its tuition over 20%. Just imagine the savings if you had prepaid the tuition before the increase. The risk of prepaying tuition is that the person may choose not to go to college, not attend that state's college system, or the college may cease to exist. Many prepaid tuition programs offer refunds. Make sure you read the refund policy of the prepaid program you are interested in obtaining. Prepaid tuition plans mainly cover tuition costs. You still need to save through other investment programs to cover additional expenses. Some prepay tuition plans will only allow you to prepay if the student is in the 10th grade or lower.

**Roth IRA**—You can use a Roth IRA to save for a wide variety of things. Every dollar you invest can be withdrawn at any time, tax-free. The gains can be withdrawn tax-free if the account has been opened for five years, and the account owner is over age 59 ½, disabled, or deceased. You can use it to save for both your retirement and your child's education. Dedicate the Roth IRA contributions to your child's education and the gains to your retirement. This works great for grandparents who are still working and want to help with their grandchildren's education.

Regardless of age, you can still withdraw contributions and gains without a tax penalty, if the distribution is for designated qualified education expenses. If you do not meet the qualifications for tax-free withdrawals, then the gains will be taxed as income. There are contribution limits and not everyone is eligible (see the next chapter for more information on the Roth IRA). Coverdell Education Savings Account (formerly called an Education IRA). In the Coverdell Education Savings Account the student is the owner. The custodian (which is usually you) maintains control of the Coverdell Education Savings Account until the student is no longer considered a minor (usually age 18 or 21, depending on the state in which the account was opened).

**Coverdell Education Savings Account**—This is great for the child's pre-college education costs (private kindergarten all the way to private high school). The Coverdell Education Savings Account gives you the flexibility in choosing and changing investment options as often as you wish. Some of the disadvantages of the Coverdell Education Savings Account are: (1) A low yearly contribution limit ($2,000 for year 2004); (2) the beneficiary assumes control of the account once he/she is no longer legally considered a minor and this could lower the amount of need-based financial aid the beneficiary could possibly receive; (3) In the year 2004, the amount you can contribute is phased out for unmarried individuals with incomes between $95,000 and $110,000 and for married couples with incomes between $190,000 and $220,000.

**Custodial Minor's Account (UGMA/UTMA)**—In this type of account...If the minor is younger than age 14, then the first $800 in unearned income is not subject to Federal income taxes. The next $800 of unearned income is taxed at the child's rate. Any unearned income of more than $1,600 is taxed at the greater of the child's or parent's marginal tax bracket. If the child is age 14 or older, any unearned income is taxed at the child's tax rate. Sometimes the child's tax rate is lower than your tax rate. That is why if you have appreciated investments, you may want to give them to your child and sell them at the child's tax rate. There are major challenges with this approach. It can hinder your child from receiving financial aid for college. You no longer own the investment. The child owns it. Therefore, it must be used for the child. In addition, the government limits the amount you can give to your child by imposing a gift tax on contributions over $11,000 as of 2004.

**Savings Bonds and I Bonds**—Savings Bonds and I-Bonds are a safe way to save for college education, and the gains may be tax-free. For more information visit website:

www.publicdebt.treas.gov/sav/saveduca.htm

These are just a few of the tax-advantaged accounts available. To learn more about other types of accounts available visit these websites:

www.collegesavings.org/planning/general.htm

www.collegeboard.com/article/0,3868,6-29-0-395,00.html

www.savingforcollege.com

## Which types of accounts seem the most appealing to your situation?

☐  Prepay Tuition
☐  Roth IRA
☐  Coverdell Education Savings Account
☐  Custodial Minor's Account (UGMA/UTMA)
☐  Savings Bonds and I-Bonds
☐  _____

# Financial Help

Scholarships are a valuable resource to pay for a child's education. Most think that only the very poor, bright, or athletic get scholarships. That is not true. There are many types of scholarships. Before you borrow money for college, you need to explore all your options.

Sure it is going to take time, but so does working a decade to pay off your college loans. Here are some suggestions:

• Visit web-based scholarship search engines like:

> www.embark.com

> www.salliemae.com

> www.collegenet.com

> www.collegequest.com

> www.scholarshipcoach.com

> www.collegeboard.org/fundfinder/html/ssrchtop.html

• Learn more about financial aid:

> www.finaid.org

> www.fafsa.ed.gov

> www.ed.gov/offices/OPE/express.html

• Look into the Federal Work Study Program or military services. As of 2004, the Federal Government does offer some tax breaks to help you afford college.

There is the Hope Scholarship Credit, in which you can receive a tax credit per child for the first two years of post-secondary or certificate education (100% of the first $1,000 in tuition and fees, 50% of the next $1,000 in tuition and fees paid).

There is the Lifetime Learning Credit in which you can receive a tax credit for 20% of qualified tuition and fees with a maximum of $2,000 per family. You cannot take both tax credits on the same person in one year.

The Hope Scholarship Credit and Lifetime Learning Credit is phased out for 2004 between adjusted gross incomes of $42,000 to $52,000 for singles, and $85,000 to $105,000 for joint returns.

To find out if you are eligible for the tax credits and other education tax breaks, read IRS Publication 970 (Tax Benefits for Education). You can find the IRS Publication 970 at their website:

www.irs.gov/pub/irs-pdf/p970.pdf

# TAX-ADVANTAGED RETIREMENT SAVINGS

Most people in retirement want around 75% of their pre-retirement income. This table will help you estimate the total nest egg you will need to provide 75% of your current salary for a 25-year retirement that begins at age 65: Select your current age and current salary that best fits your situation.

For example... Age: 60        Current Salary: $60,000
Retirement Income:    $45,000        ($60,000 X 75%)
That person will need an estimated $712,000 for retirement.

| Current Salary (CS) | $20,000 | $40,000 | $60,000 |
|---|---|---|---|
| CS After 75% | $15,000 | $30,000 | $45,000 |
| **Age** | | | |
| 20 | $1,252,000 | $2,606,000 | $3,963,000 |
| 25 | $1,010,000 | $2,120,000 | $3,233,000 |
| 30 | $813,000 | $1,722,000 | $2,633,000 |
| 35 | $651,000 | $1,395,000 | $2,142,000 |
| 40 | $511,000 | $1,116,000 | $1,724,000 |
| 45 | $409,000 | $897,000 | $1,395,000 |
| 50 | $326,000 | $719,000 | $1,126,000 |
| 55 | $258,000 | $572,000 | $905,000 |
| 60 | $195,000 | $442,000 | $712,000 |

These calculations are estimates only. They assume a 4% inflation rate, 8% investment return and have the principal depleted after 25 years. No tax consequences were considered. All returns and inflations rate are hypothetical and are not intended to represent the performance of any specific investment. As always investing involves risks and you may incur a profit or a loss.

| Current Salary (CS) | $80,000 | $100,000 | $120,000 |
|---|---|---|---|
| CS After 75% | $60,000 | $75,000 | $90,000 |

| Age | | | |
|---|---|---|---|
| 20 | $5,322,000 | $6,681,000 | $8,541,000 |
| 25 | $4,347,000 | $5,460,000 | $6,575,000 |
| 30 | $3,546,000 | $4,459,000 | $5,373,000 |
| 35 | $2,890,000 | $3,637,000 | $4,386,000 |
| 40 | $2,334,000 | $2,944,000 | $3,555,000 |
| 45 | $1,894,000 | $2,393,000 | $2,893,000 |
| 50 | $1,534,000 | $1,942,000 | $2,351,000 |
| 55 | $1,238,000 | $1,572,000 | $1,906,000 |
| 60 | $983,000 | $1,253,000 | $1,524,000 |

These calculations are estimates only. They assume a 4% inflation rate, 8% investment return and have the principal depleted after 25 years. No tax consequences were considered. All returns and inflations rate are hypothetical and are not intended to represent the performance of any specific investment. As always investing involves risks and you may incur a profit or a loss.

For your own personalized calculation go to Kiplinger's website and look for Managing Retirement (www.kiplinger.com/tools).

There are many tax-advantaged retirement savings accounts. The starting point for most employed people should be their company's retirement plan, especially if the company matches your contributions. That is free money! Let us assume that your company matches up to 6% of your pay for every dollar you contribute. If you contribute up to the 6% match then that is like getting a 6% raise or 100% rate of return on your money. Plus, it saves you money on your taxes and 12% of your salary is invested yearly for your retirement.

# Roth IRA

Once you contribute up to the maximum your company matches, where else can you invest for retirement? The Roth IRA! Unlike most retirement accounts, the Roth IRA does not give you a tax deduction for contributing to it; however, it grows tax-free and comes out tax-free at retirement (as long as you are over age 59 ½ and the Roth IRA account has been open for at least five years). The disadvantages of the Roth IRA are: In 2005, you can contribute only $4,000 yearly or $4,500 if age 50 or older. The contribution limit is planned to increase over time. Not everyone can have a Roth IRA. There are income requirements and restrictions. You can contribute up to the combined amount of earned income (W-2 or net self-employed income) that you or your spouse has made for that year. Therefore, if you and your spouse are not employed then you cannot contribute.

You cannot contribute if you make too much:
A single person with a modified Adjusted Gross Income (AGI) over $110,000 or a married couple filing jointly with a modified AGI over $160,000 cannot contribute to a Roth IRA. You can contribute the full amount if you are single and your modified AGI is less than $95,000, or if you are married, filing jointly, and your AGI is less than $150,000. You can do a partial contribution if you are single, earning $95,000 to $109,999, or married filing jointly, earning $150,000 to $159,999.

Because our government has imposed a marginal tax system, it is important for you to know the rules and avoid mistakes that can place you into a higher tax bracket. By contributing to a tax-deductible retirement plan, you reduce your current tax liability. In theory, at retirement, everything will be paid off (no mortgage, no car payments, and no more having to save for retirement and the children's college) and with fewer financial obligations your income requirements are less. Thus, you may be in a lower tax bracket during retirement. In theory, this may be true. In reality, some people at retirement will continue to be in the same income tax bracket because of their personal income requirements or income from sources like pensions, dividends, and interest. For others, by the time they retire they may be in a higher tax bracket due to the government increasing taxes to support the programs like Social Security, Medicare, etc.

You have more tax control with a Roth IRA because qualified withdrawals from a Roth IRA account are federally income tax-free. For example, Tom is now 59 ½ and ready to retire. He made a qualified withdrawal of $50,000 from his Roth IRA federally income tax-free to pay off his house and car. By eliminating his car and house payments, his income need is reduced. Thus, he is able to live comfortably in a lower tax bracket. If he withdrew $50,000 from a 401k or Traditional IRA, a large proportion would be lost to taxes.

# Traditional IRA

You can contribute to both a Roth IRA and a Traditional IRA; however, the combined total contributions cannot exceed $4,000 ($4,500 if age 50 or older). There are times when a Traditional IRA is the better choice than a Roth IRA. For Example:

- If you have a large retirement account from a previous employer and you want to transfer it into an IRA, then use the Traditional IRA to help defer taxes longer.

- If you will be in a lower income tax bracket at retirement and you qualify for a tax deduction on a Traditional IRA contribution, then use a Traditional IRA.

- If you make too much income to qualify for a Roth IRA, then the Traditional IRA is a good choice to grow your retirement investments tax-deferred.

The amount that can be contributed for 2005 is 100% of your or your spouse's earned income with a maximum of $4,000 per person ($4,500 if age 50 or older). There is no minimum age for making a Traditional IRA contribution, but there is a maximum age of 70 ½. It is important to note that earned income means income received from working. It does not include the income from investments.

In 2004, if you are covered by an employer-sponsored plan, the amount you can deduct for a Traditional IRA contribution is determined by the amount of modified adjusted gross income you make:

| | Full Deduction | Partial Deduction | No Deduction |
|---|---|---|---|
| Single filing status: | < than $45,000 | $45,000 to $50,000 | > than $55,000 |
| Married filing jointly: | <than $65,000 | $65,000 to $75,000 | > than $75,000 |

For those not covered by an employer-sponsored plan, but filing a joint return with a spouse who is covered by an employer-sponsored plan, the phase-out range for deducting a 2004 contribution to a Traditional IRA is $150,000 to $160,000.

Check with your tax advisor to see which IRA is best for you. For more information read IRS Publication 590 or visit the IRS website:

www.irs.gov/pub/irs-pdf/p590.pdf

To learn more about small business retirement plans read IRS Publication 560 or visit the IRS website:

www.irs.gov/pub/irs-pdf/p560.pdf

# Annuity

Annuities are designed to be used for retirement. One of the most popular advantages is their tax-deferred growth. By deferring taxes until retirement, there is the potential that withdrawals from your annuity will be taxed at a lower rate than during your working years due to lower income. However, tax rates can always change and may be higher. With a non-qualified annuity, withdrawals are taxable only to the extent they are considered gains.

You insure your house, your car, and other valuables. Why not insure your investments? Annuities are issued by insurance companies and offer various guarantees like income protection, death benefits, and guarantee of principal. Because of the insurance aspect of annuities, some people prefer to have their Roth IRA or Traditional IRA in annuities. It is important to note that the guarantees are based on the claims paying ability of the insurance company.

Annuities, with designated beneficiaries, avoid probate and pass directly to the beneficiaries. Some annuities allow you to determine how the beneficiaries will receive the annuity proceeds like lump-sum distribution, proceeds paid over a period of time, and lifetime payout. This feature is especially important for those who are concerned about their beneficiaries' abilities to manage money.

There are some disadvantages of annuities. With few exceptions, there is an IRS 10% penalty on taxable withdrawals for those who are younger than 59 ½. Gains on an annuity are taxed as ordinary income, instead of capital gains. Ordinary income taxes are usually taxed at a higher percentage rate than capital gains' tax rates. Since annuities are not subject to capital gains, they do not receive the step-up or step-down in cost basis at death.

If your insurance company becomes insolvent, you can lose all or part of your investment depending on what type of annuity it is. Some states have a Guaranty Association that offers certain principle guarantees just in case an insurance company becomes insolvent. However, not all types of annuities are covered by the Guaranty Association, and the guarantee has a limit. The limit varies based on the state in which you are legally considered a resident. To find out more about the Guaranty Association check with your State's Department of Insurance or visit this website:

www.nolhga.com/stateinformation/main.cfm

# Cash-Value Life Insurance

Another tax-advantaged vehicle for retirement is cash-value life insurance. It is life insurance with investment(s) that are professionally managed. It can provide tax-deferred growth (Theodore H. Cohen 39 TC 1055 (1963), acq 1964-1 CB-4), income tax-free death benefits (IRC Sec. 101), and tax-advantaged income (IRC Sec. 7702). If used incorrectly, it can be a poor use of investment dollars. In most cases, the initial cost for cash-value life insurance is high. To receive the best benefit, you need to:

(1)  contribute the maximum allowed by the government without turning it into a Modified Endowment Contract (MEC);

(2)  have the account open for at least 15 years before making withdrawals;

(3)  never let the policy be canceled. You must always have enough money to pay for the cost of the life insurance.

If you are unwilling or unable to commit to these three guidelines, then do not use cash-value life insurance as a supplemental retirement vehicle (These are generalizations and not always true in every situation).

If you contribute too much or withdraw contributions too soon, it could turn your life insurance policy into a Modified Endowment Contract (MEC), meaning the policy loses some of its tax-advantages and may incur a tax penalty on past, current, or future withdrawals from the policy.

The investment part of the life insurance contract (called cash value) grows tax-deferred. Internal Revenue Code (IRC) Section 7702 states that as long as the life insurance contract is not a MEC then the first money to be withdrawn from the life insurance policy is a return of your contributions; thus, it is not taxable. However, withdrawals potentially can be subject to early withdrawal penalties by the insurance company. The same Internal

Revenue Code (IRC) Section 7702 states that the policy owner can borrow most of the money from the investment part of the contract and be free from taxation as long as the policy is not canceled or does not become an MEC.

You might be saying, "Why would I want to borrow?" The answer is taxes! If you invest $30,000 into your cash-value life insurance policy and over time it grows to $130,000, then $30,000 comes out tax-free as a return of your contribution. Any withdrawals of the gains would be subject to income taxes, plus an IRS 10% penalty if it is a MEC and the owner of

the policy is under the age of 59 ½. If you borrow it and it is not a MEC, you avoid the taxes and early withdrawal penalties; however, the loan has to be repaid. You may be asking, "How am I going to pay it back?" This is life insurance. When you die, your life insurance proceeds will repay the loan INCOME TAX-FREE.

Most insurance companies charge a low interest rate on their policy loans. Some have a net cost of 0%. Let me explain through an example: The insurance company loans you $10,000 from your cash value inside your life insurance contract. The insurance company charges you a 5% interest rate. For collateral like purposes, they hold $10,000 from your cash value account in a fixed account paying 5%. If they charge 5% and you earn 5%, what is the cost of the loan? 0%! If all works as planned, your investment grows tax-free and produces a tax-free income in the form of a loan. When you die, an income tax-free death benefit pays off the loan and the balance of the death benefit transfers income tax-free to your beneficiaries.

Cash-value life insurance provides great tax-advantaged benefits. So, why doesn't everyone do this? Insurance costs! If you are unhealthy, the insurance cost is probably too high to make this an effective insurance/investment product. Using cash-value life insurance to supplement retirement requires a lifetime commitment. You have to overfund it for a long period of time to make it effective, and you cannot cancel it.

For example, you invest $30,000 into cash-value life insurance, and over time it grows to $130,000. You withdraw $30,000 and borrow $90,000. Ten years later you decide to cancel the policy. The $90,000 debt, plus interest, and any other gains will be subject to income taxes. What if you did not cancel it? You may have another problem. Remember, this is life insurance and there is a cost. The insurance company can raise the internal cost of the insurance, and you have no control over that. There is usually a limit to how much they can increase the insurance cost. Over time, due to the insurance cost, the $10,000 left in the account may disappear. As you get older, the insurance cost may become too expensive to afford. Unless you can pay the current insurance cost, the policy will be canceled.

Hopefully, you have a better understanding why this can be a dangerous retirement vehicle if not used properly. As a result, this strategy is only for a very select group of people.

# Warning about Retirement Accounts

It is important to know that most tax-advantaged retirement accounts like IRAs, 401k, 403b, and annuities have a 10% IRS withdrawal penalty if not used for retirement or specific government-defined uses. For most retirement accounts, the eligible retirement age is 59 ½ or older. If you want to retire before age 59 ½ and avoid the IRS 10% withdrawal penalty on your retirement account, then you need to use the IRS 72T calculation to determine the amount of income you can receive yearly from your retirement account.

The amount of income you can receive from an IRS 72T calculation is based on your account balance, expected investment return, and life expectancy. Once you start taking the income, you cannot stop it until you have received the income for at least five years and you are over age 59 ½. The thought process of the IRS is if you are truly retired then you will need an income for life. As a general rule of thumb, the younger you are, the smaller the income you will be allowed to receive according to the IRS 72T calculations. Your company retirement plan may allow for an early retirement at age 55. To find out, check with your human resources director or read your company's retirement plan document.

**What type of tax-advantaged retirement account would work best for you?**

☐  **Roth IRA**
☐  **Traditional IRA**
☐  **Annuity**
☐  **Cash-Value Life Insurance**
☐  **Company Sponsored Retirement Plan (401k, SEP, etc.)**
☐  _____

# THE BEST INVESTMENT

"…store up for yourselves treasures in heaven…" (Matthew 6:19).

So far we have talked about temporary investments and estate planning. They are temporary in comparison with eternity. That is why we believe that the best investment and estate planning you can make for your family and yourself is to invest your life in Christ. Invest your life in the things that are eternal. Jesus said, "…store up for yourselves treasures in heaven where moth and rust do not destroy, and where thieves do not break in and steal. For where your treasure is, there your heart will be also" (Mat. 6:19-21, NIV).

Have you ever heard, "It is not what you know, it's who you know that counts"? In fact, you probably have experienced it. It is the same way with getting into Heaven. It is not about how smart and good you are that allows you to enter into Heaven. It is about receiving God's gift of salvation and having a personal relationship with God. There is a myth that states that good people go to heaven and bad people go to hell. That is true to an extent. By spending time with God your heart changes and you start doing the things that honor God. However, you can never be good enough to get into heaven. You need God's grace that unmerited favor and gift of salvation.

You can preach and perform miracles in God's name, but if you don't have a close relationship with God and His family, you're not going to Heaven, as seen in this scripture: "Not everyone who says to me, 'Lord, Lord,' will enter the kingdom of heaven, but only he who does the will of my Father who is in heaven. Many will say to me on that day, 'Lord, Lord, did we not prophesy in your name, and in your name drive out demons and perform many miracles?' Then I will tell them plainly, 'I never knew you. Away from me, you evildoers!'"(Mat. 7:21-23, NIV). How do you know God's will for you? By having a relationship with Him!

## Are you too busy doing things for God, instead of doing things with God?

"For He chose us in Him before the creation of the world to be holy and blameless in his sight. In love, He predestined us to be adopted as His sons through Jesus Christ, in accordance with His pleasure and will—to the praise of His glorious grace, which He has freely given us in the One He loves. In Him we have redemption through His blood, the forgiveness of sins, in accordance with the riches of God's grace that He lavished on us with all wisdom and understanding. With all wisdom and understanding, He made known to us the mystery of His will according to His good pleasure, which He purposed in Christ, to be put into effect when the times will have reached their fulfillment—to bring all things in heaven and on earth together under one head, even Christ. In Him we were also chosen, having been predestined according to the plan of Him who works out everything in conformity with the purpose of His will, in order that we, who were the first to hope in Christ, might be for the praise of His glory. And you also were included in Christ when you heard the word of truth, the gospel of your salvation. Having believed, you were marked in Him with a seal, the promised Holy Spirit, who is a deposit guaranteeing our inheritance until the redemption of those who are God's possession—to the praise of his glory" (Eph. 1:4-14, NIV).

Wouldn't it be a tragedy if God says to you, "I never knew you." I never want you to hear those words from Him. It is extremely important for you to receive God's gift of salvation and develop your relationship with Him.

Jesus said, "'Do not work for food that spoils, but for food that endures to eternal life, which the Son of Man will give you....'...The work of God is this: to believe in the one He has sent...For my Father's will is that everyone who looks to the Son and believes in him shall have eternal life, and I will raise him up at the last day'" (John 6:27-40, NIV).

**We are all going to live somewhere after we die. It is either going to be heaven or hell. Where will you be?** Jesus said, "If you really knew me, you would know {God} as well...Because I live, you also will live...whoever has my commands and obeys them, he is the one who loves me. He who loves me will be loved by my Father, and I too will love him..." (John 14:7-21, NIV). "[God] is able to do immeasurably more than all we ask or imagine, according to his power that is at work within us, to Him be glory in the church and in Christ Jesus throughout all generations, forever and ever! Amen" (Eph. 3:20-21, NIV).

**When are you ever good enough to get into heaven? Are you truly a good person?**
Jesus said, "'No one [is] good but One, [that] [is], God. But if you want to enter into life, keep the commandments...If you want to be perfect, go, sell what you have and give to the poor, and you will have treasure in heaven; and come, follow Me...When His disciples heard [it], they were greatly astonished, saying, 'Who then can be saved?' But Jesus looked at [them] and said to them, 'With men this is impossible, but with God all things are possible'" (Mat. 19:17-26). Jesus said, "I am the way, the truth, and the life. No one comes to the Father except through Me"(John 14:6). Christianity is the only major religion in the world that provides the unmerited gift of the forgiveness of sins and eternal life (Eph. 1:6,7; 2:8) and a personal relationship with its founder (John 4:42; 2 Tim. 1:12). God is reaching down to you and out of His loving kindness and grace He offers mercy and forgiveness of sins (Tit. 3:3-7). He offers forgiveness through His son so that you are able to develop a close relationship with Him.

# Creation

The greatest evidence that God is alive is His creation.

"All of creation declares there is a God" (Rom. 1:20, NIV).

It is not logically possible for us to have been accidentally created. Look at nature and how complex every living thing is, and you will know, without a doubt, there is a God. Even for the theory of evolution to work, God has to intervene to help things evolve. The mathematical probability that after billions of billions of years of random mutation and nature selection ultimately produced a human or any other complex animal is beyond sound mind and reason. A mutation of any kind is almost always harmful to an organism. The probability of having beneficial mutations to form a single-celled organism eventually evolving into a human is impossible.

The Second Law of Thermodynamics states that matter and energy always tend to change from complex and ordered states to disordered states; thus, acknowledging that complex forms do not just naturally develop or evolve without a force causing it to change.

Other evidence that God is alive is the change that takes place in people who have a close relationship with God through Jesus. "Therefore if any man be in Christ, he is a new creature: old things are passed away; behold, all things are become new"
(2 Cor. 5:17, KJV).

I suggest reading John 1:5; 2 Cor. 2:14; Luke 24:45; and John 16:13. Go to www.crosswalk.com to read the Bible for free.

*Do you have a relationship with God
through Jesus Christ?*

*If not, then it is time to start.*

# Developing a Relationship with God

According to Dr. James Kennedy, the Bible has over two thousand prophecies and over half of them have come true. No other book can claim this. Yet as powerful as it is, you can read the Bible backwards and forwards, know it by heart, and not know God. You will know of Him, but you will never know Him until you experience a personal relationship with Him. Developing a relationship with Him is like most relationships. It takes time, effort, and trust. It is a fact of life that we make time for the things we truly love. God should be at the top of our list. The great thing about God is no matter where you are, there He is. You can communicate any time with Him and with your eyes open or shut.

The Bible is a great way to learn about God, and it enhances your relationship with God. The benefits are tremendous when you dig for the deep truths about God (Ps. 119:10-11), "and store up [God's] commands within" (Prov. 2:1, NIV) and "lay hold of God's words with all your heart" (Prov. 4:4, NIV).

Everyone should have someone he or she can meet with each week, either in person or over the phone to share experiences and ideas, to pray for, and encourage.

Jesus replied: "'Love the Lord your God with all your heart and with all your soul and with all your mind.' This is the first and greatest commandment. And the second is like it: 'Love your neighbor as yourself.' All the Law and the Prophets hang on these two commandments" (Mat. 22:37-40).

You should begin your journey by reading all of the New Testament. Begin at the first book, the book of Matthew. The Bible is designed to be placed into your heart, soul, and mind, and into action. That is why you should read about one chapter per day. After you read the chapter, review it, meditate on it throughout the day, and place it in your heart. Jesus said the most important thing in life is to have a committed, whole-hearted, loving relationship with God. That is why God gave us salvation, so that we can forever have a relationship with Him.

To have a better understanding of this relationship, when the New Testament references information about God's relationship with you, mark it with the symbol of the cross. The second most important thing is to love others as you love yourself. Thus, everywhere you see in the scriptures about how to love others, mark it with a heart. Everywhere it talks about the financial aspects of life, mark it with a dollar symbol. To learn more about God, go to www.crosswalk.com, www.seacoast.org, and visit a local church.

*"That if you confess with your mouth, 'Jesus is Lord', and believe in your heart that God raised him from the dead, you will be saved. For it is with your heart that you believe and are justified, and it is with your mouth that you confess and are saved" (Romans 10:9-10).*

**I confess that Jesus is my Lord and Savior.**

_____ *(signature)*

_____ *(signature)*

_____ *(date)*

We pray this book accomplished its mission in your life. If this book has inspired you or helped you in any way, please let us know. We value the encouragement. If we can be of service to your ministry or organization, we can be reached at

**Alpha Omega Financial Ministries**
(843) 270-6618

# GENERAL RECOMMENDATION CHECKLIST

## Budget

☐  Develop and follow a Savings & Spending Plan (Budget).
☐  Start an allowance program.

☐  _____.

☐  _____.

## Emergency Fund

☐  Save the equivalent of 4 to 8 months of living expenses in a bank money market.
☐  Obtain a line of credit that can be used for financial emergencies.

☐  _____.

☐  _____.

# Financial Planning

- ☐ Use financial calculators to estimate how much you should be saving to reach your financial goals: www.kiplinger.com/tools, cgi.money.cnn.com/tools, etc.
- ☐ Hire a professional to help you create your plan
  - ☐ CERTIFIED FINANCIAL PLANNER™ Professional
  - ☐ _____
- ☐ Find a Financial Coach

- ☐ _____.

- ☐ _____.

# Estate Planning

- ☐ Update your estate plan (Will, trust(s), power of attorney, Living Will, etc.) to effectively transfer wealth, minimize cost, and reduce hassle.
- ☐ Consider the advisability of having a Will or reviewing your Will.
- ☐ Obtain Pre-Paid Legal Services®, Inc. coverage to receive a Will, certain coverage, and discounts.
- ☐ Consider the advantages of a trust.
- ☐ Obtain a family lawyer software program.
- ☐ Coordinate your trust with your Will.
- ☐ Consult your attorney about reviewing your trust and Will.
- ☐ Consider the advantages of starting a Limited Partnership.
- ☐ Review how you hold title to your various assets.
- ☐ Update the beneficiaries on all accounts (life insurance, IRAs, Transfer on Death, etc.).
- ☐ Make it easy for your estate executor to find and obtain the necessary documents.

☐ _____.

☐ _____.

# Insurance Planning

☐ Increase the amount of life insurance so that upon one's death, the proceeds will pay off all debt and provide for those who are dependent on you.

☐ Update the insurance coverage on your
    ☐ spouse     ☐ own life

☐ Disability insurance.-
    ☐ Purchase     ☐ Increase coverage     ☐ _____

☐ Long-term care insurance-
    ☐ Purchase     ☐ Increase coverage     ☐ _____

☐ Health insurance-
    ☐ Purchase     ☐ Increase coverage     ☐ _____

☐ Incorporate the common disaster provision in your insurance policy.

☐ Have your Property, Casualty, & Liability agent to review your coverage.

☐ _____.

☐ _____.

# Debt Elimination Planning

☐ Make the minimum payments on all other debts and focus mainly on paying off the debt you owe to a family member or friend.

☐ Refinance your house at a lower interest rate.

☐ Pay extra towards the principle of your house.

☐ Invest in a Roth IRA for five years or longer and when you are older than 59 ½ use part of its cash accumulation to pay off your house.

☐ Refinance your home to receive cash to pay off all your credit cards.

☐ Pay off your credit card balances before you receive a finance charge.

☐ Consolidate debt with a low interest rate loan.

☐ Prioritize debt: family loans, highest interest rate debt, or debts with very low balances should be paid off first.

☐ Refinance your credit card by calling your credit card company and ask for a lower rate to match the deals you have received in the mail from other credit companies. If they do not comply, then transfer the debt to another credit card.

☐ Use EverydayWealth services to monitor your credit and follow their plan for becoming debt free. Visit website www.wealthlink.com/planner to enroll.

☐ Program into your cell phone all your credit card phone numbers just in case they are stolen. Carry a list of your credit card phone numbers in your car. Do not include the account numbers.

☐ Review your free annual credit reports through www.annualcreditreport.com

☐ _____.

☐ _____.

# General Investment Planning

- ☐ Review your investment portfolio.
- ☐ Reallocate and diversify investments to match your goals with your risk tolerance.
- ☐ Diversify through a variety of assets, managers, and styles.
- ☐ Consider reallocating your investments by
  ☐ increasing ☐ decreasing holdings in _____
- ☐ Consider reallocating your investments by
  ☐ increasing ☐ decreasing holdings in _____
- ☐ Consider reallocating your investments by
  ☐ increasing ☐ decreasing holdings in _____
- ☐ Diversify your income sources:
  ☐ Start a business
  ☐ Get a part-time job.
  ☐ _____

- ☐ _____.

- ☐ _____.

# College Planning

- ☐ To save for _____ college use a _____.
- ☐ To save for _____ college use a Coverdell Education Savings Account.
- ☐ To save for _____ college use a Prepaid tuition plan.
- ☐ To save for _____ college use a Custodial Minor's Account.
- ☐ To save for _____ college use a Trust.
- ☐ To save for _____ use a _____ IRA.
- ☐ Use a Roth IRA to save both for college (your contribution) and for retirement (gains after 59 1/2).

☐ Search for scholarships: www.collegequest.com, www.scholarship-coach.com, etc.

☐ Obtain financial aid: www.finaid.org, www.fafsa.ed.gov, etc.

☐ _____.

☐ _____.

☐ _____.

☐ _____.

☐ _____.

☐ _____.

# Retirement Planning

☐ Diversify by transferring certain investments into an annuity with a living benefit.

☐ Contribute up to the company's match in the retirement program at work.

☐ Use tax-advantage accounts for retirement (Roth IRA, Traditional IRA, Annuity, Cash-Value Life Insurance, 401k, SEP, SIMPLE IRA, etc.).

☐ Consider investing the maximum amount you can contribute into a Roth IRA.

☐ Consider the establishment of a
    ☐ SEP      ☐ SIMPLE      ☐ 401k      ☐_____.
    Consider revising your
    ☐ SEP      ☐ SIMPLE      ☐ 401k      ☐_____.

☐ Review the funding arrangement of your retirement plan.

☐ _____.

☐ _____.

☐ _____.

☐ _____.

☐ _____.

☐ _____.

☐ _____.

# Eternal Planning

☐ Develop a closer relationship with God by…
- ☐ Communicating daily with God (prayer).
- ☐ Trusting God more.
- ☐ Praying for others and myself.
- ☐ Experiencing God through His people by attending a church and _____.
- ☐ Sharing Jesus with others.

☐ Experiencing and doing both individual and group worship.
☐ Ministering to others.
☐ Reflecting God's character through my life.
☐ Reading and studying all of the
- ☐ New Testament     ☐ Old Testament.

☐ _____.

☐ _____.

☐ _____.

☐ _____.

☐ _____.

☐ _____.

☐ _____.

☐ _____.

# FAVORITE WEBSITES

## Becoming A Business Owner

EverydayWealth
>www.wealthlink.com/planner

IRS—Business Use of Your Home
>www.irs.gov/pub/irs-pdf/p587.pdf

IRS—Home-Based Businesses
>www.irs.gov/pub/irs-pdf/p4035.pdf

IRS—Retirement Plans for Small Business
>www.irs.gov/pub/irs-pdf/p560.pdf

IRS—Small Business Resource
>www.irs.gov/businesses/small/index.html

IRS—Tax Guide For Small Business
>www.irs.gov/pub/irs-pdf/p334.pdf

IRS—Travel, Entertainment, Gift, and Car Expenses
>www.irs.gov/pub/irs-pdf/p463.pdf

US Tax Codes
>www.fourmilab.ch/ustax

## Budget Calculators

Ideal Budget
>cgi.money.cnn.com/tools/budget101/budget_101.jsp

In-depth Budget
>www.kiplinger.com/tools/budget.html

Simple Budget
www.calcbuilder.com/cgi-bin/calcs/BUD3.cgi/Kiplinger

# Calculators

Bankrate.com Calculators
    www.bankrate.com/brm/rate/calc_home.asp
CNN Money Calculators
    cgi.money.cnn.com/tools/
Kiplinger Calculators
    www.kiplinger.com/tools/
MSN Money Calculators
    moneycentral.msn.com/help/tools.asp
Turbo Tax Calculators
    www.turbotax.com/calculators/index.html

# Car

Home equity loan or auto loan for a car
    www.calcbuilder.com/cgi-bin/calcs/AUT8.cgi/Kiplinger
Kiplinger.com Car Finder
    www.kiplinger.com/tools/carfinder/
Should I lease or purchase
    www.calcbuilder.com/cgi-bin/calcs/AUT3.cgi/Kiplinger
Which is better-a new or used car
    www.calcbuilder.com/cgi-bin/calcs/AUT1.cgi/Kiplinger

# Career Planning

Average salary for your job in your area of the country
    salary.money.cnn.com/

Cost of Living comparison between two cities
        cgi.money.cnn.com/tools/costofliving/costofliving.html
Hot Jobs (job search)
        hotjobs.yahoo.com/
Match your personality with a career
        www.crown.org/tools/personality_instructions.asp
Monster (job search)
        www.monster.com/

# Christianity

Bible Study Tools
        www.crosswalk.com/
Bible Study Tools
        www.biblegateway.com
Christianity.com
        home.christianity.com
Financial Library
        www.crown.org/library
Music (radio)104.7 The Fish
        www.thefishatlanta.com
Music—Worship Together Home Page
        www.worshiptogether.com
Seacoast Church—Message
        www.seacoast.org/mountpleasant

# College Planning

CNNmoney
        money.cnn.com/pf/college
College Board
        www.collegeboard.com

College Savings Calculator—CNNmoney
        cgi.money.cnn.com/tools/collegeplanner/collegeplanner.jsp
CollegeNET.com
        www.collegenet.com/about/index_htm
FAFSA—Federal Student Aid
        www.ed.gov/about/offices/list/fsa/index.html
U.S. Dept. of Education
        www.fafsa.ed.gov/what010.htm


SmartStudent Guide to Financial Aid
        www.finaid.org
Peterson's Colleges and Universities
        www.petersons.com/ugchannel
Sallie Mae
        www.salliemae.com
Savings Bonds for Education
        www.publicdebt.treas.gov/sav/saveduca.htm
Savingforcollege.com LLC.
        www.savingforcollege.com
Scholarship Search
        apps.collegeboard.com/cbsearch_ss/scholarshipSearch.jsp
ScholarshipCoach.com
        www.scholarshipcoach.com
State College Savings Plans—Kiplingers
www.kiplinger.com/tools/managing/college/savings/2001/states01.html
Tax Benefits for Education
        www.irs.gov/pub/irs-pdf/p970.pdf
The Princeton Review
        www.princetonreview.com/?popup=yes
Top 100 Values in Public Colleges Kiplinger.com
        www.kiplinger.com/personalfinance/tools/colleges/
What Is the Payoff for Going Back to School
        www.kiplinger.com/tools/managing/college/gradschool.html

# Debt Elimination Planning

Consumer Credit Counseling Service
www.cccsatl.org
Credit Bureau—Equifax
www.equifax.com
Credit Bureau—Experian
www.experian.com
Credit Bureau—TransUnion Corporation
www.tuc.com
Debt Reduction Calculator
cgi.money.cnn.com/tools/debtplanner/debtplanner.jsp
EverydayWealth
www.wealthlink.com/planner
Free Annual Credit Reports
www.annualcreditreport.com
Should I consolidate my debts
www.calcbuilder.com/cgi-bin/calcs/CRE5.cgi/Kiplinger

# Estate Planning

Estate Tax Rates & Updates
www.statefarm.com/insuranc/life/taxgone.htm
LawEasy.com
www.laweasy.com

# General Financial Information

Basics on Financial Management
www.kiplinger.com/basics
Bloomberg financial markets news
www.bloomberg.com

Financial Library
>   www.crown.org/library

Find a CFP® Professional
>   www.fpanet.org/PlannerSearch

MarketWatch (CBS)
>   www.marketwatch.com

MSN Money
>   moneycentral.msn.com

Morningstar Research
>   www.morningstar.com

Money 101
>   money.cnn.com/pf/101/lessons/1/index.html

Quicken.com
>   www.quicken.com

Social Security Online
>   www.ssa.gov

USA Today
>   www.usatoday.com

Wall Street Journal
>   online.wsj.com/public/us

# Insurance Planning

Guaranty Association
>   www.nolhga.com/stateinformation/main.cfm

Insurance Planner
>   moneycentral.msn.com/insure/welcome.asp

Life Insurance Calculator
>   www.calcbuilder.com/cgi-bin/calcs/INS1.cgi/Kiplinger

Long-term Care Costs for your area of the country
>   cgi.money.cnn.com/tools/elder_care/elder_care_cost_finder.html

# Safety Rating of Insurance Company

A.M. Best
www.ambest.com/index.htm
Duff & Phelps
www.dufflle.com
Moody
www.moodys.com
Weiss
www.weissratings.com

# Mortgage Planning

15 vs. 30 year mortgage calculator
www.calcbuilder.com/cgi-bin/calcs/HOM6.cgi/Kiplinger
HomeAdvisor–MSN
moneycentral.msn.com/money/2001/redir.asp?mcrid=117
How advantageous are extra payments
www.calcbuilder.com/cgi-bin/calcs/HOM16.cgi/Kiplinger
How much will my home equity loan payments be
www.calcbuilder.com/cgi-bin/calcs/HEL4.cgi/Kiplinger
How much will my mortgage payments be
www.calcbuilder.com/cgi-bin/calcs/HOM2.cgi/Kiplinger
Mortgage Decision Making Calculators
www.bankrate.com/kip/mortgage-advisers/home.asp
Which is better fixed or adjustable
www.calcbuilder.com/cgi-bin/calcs/HOM4.cgi/Kiplinger

# Retirement Planning

Individual Retirement Accounts (IRS)
www.irs.gov/pub/irs-pdf/p590.pdf

Pensions and Annuities (IRS)
> www.irs.gov/pub/irs-pdf/p575.pdf

Retirement Plans for Small Business
> www.irs.gov/pub/irs-pdf/p560.pdf

Retirement Quick Calculator
cgi.money.cnn.com/tools/retirementneed/retirementneed_plain.html

# Taxes

Calculators (TurboTax)
> www.turbotax.com/calculators/index.html

Individual Retirement Accounts
> www.irs.gov/pub/irs-pdf/p590.pdf

IRS.gov Home
> www.irs.gov

Morningstar Tax Planning
> www.morningstar.com/centers/tax.html

Retirement Plans for Small Business
> www.irs.gov/pub/irs-pdf/p560.pdf

Tax Estimator
> moneycentral.msn.com/investor/calcs/n_tax/main.asp

U.S. Tax Code On-Line
> www.fourmilab.ch/ustax

*If legal, financial, tax or other professional advice is required, those services should be provided by an accredited and licensed advisor who can advise you on your specific needs. The advice and views expressed from these websites may be different from the views and advice Anissa and Dustin LaPorte would provide. Anissa and Dustin LaPorte cannot guarantee the accuracy of the websites, nor can Anissa and Dustin LaPorte guarantee these websites still offer their services.*

# ABOUT THE AUTHORS

For over a decade, Dustin has been helping people reach their financial goals by teaching and implementing biblically based financial principles and strategies. He is a native of the Carolinas and is a graduate of the University of North Carolina at Charlotte holding a Bachelor of Science degree in Business Administration and CERTIFIED FINANCIAL PLANNER™ designation. He also writes articles for the *Holy City Chronicle*, a popular Charleston Christian newspaper. He has conducted over a thousand one-on-one personal consultations, as well as many group seminars for various organizations and churches.

Anissa provides a unique perspective. She is a graduate of the Medical University of South Carolina. Through their years of marriage together, they have experienced the challenges and blessings of biblical based financial management. They have taken the best of what they have learned and placed it in this book for you to experience.

978-0-595-32844-4
0-595-32844-X

www.ingramcontent.com/pod-product-compliance
Lightning Source LLC
Chambersburg PA
CBHW031056180526
45163CB00002BA/852